RHYTHMS OF MARRIAGE

STRENGTHENING YOUR RELATIONSHIP
TO THE BEAT OF GOD'S DESIGN

www.rhythmsofmarriage.org

Published by Kingdom Rhythms LLC

ISBN: 979-8-9959746-0-4

Cover design by Kingdom Rhythms LLC
Interior design by Kingdom Rhythms LLC

Printed in the United States of America

About the Authors

Bill and Jennsey McGee have shared life together for more than forty years, beginning their journey as high school sweethearts and building a marriage marked by faith, perseverance, growth, and enduring love. Their story is one of learning how strong marriages are not built by accident, but through intentional rhythms practiced over time.

Bill spent twenty years in corporate world with IBM before stepping fully into ministry, where he has now served as a pastor for over twenty years. Through decades of leadership, counseling, and teaching, he has helped individuals, couples, and families pursue spiritual health and relational strength.

Jennsey served as a school teacher for thirty-two years, investing her life in students and families with wisdom, compassion, and dedication. Her heart for people, practical insight, and nurturing spirit have made her a trusted voice to countless couples navigating the joys and challenges of marriage.

Together, Bill and Jennsey have spent the last twenty-five years mentoring and coaching couples, helping them build healthier relationships, stronger communication, deeper intimacy, and Christ-centered homes. Their passion is to see marriages restored, strengthened, and equipped to thrive in every season of life.

They are parents, speakers, mentors, coaches, and encouragers for couples at every stage of the journey.

Bill and Jennsey are the proud parents of one daughter, Mallory, and remain deeply grateful for the life and legacy God has allowed them to build together.

Their message is simple: great marriages are not found—they are built, one intentional rhythm at a time.

RHYTHMS OF
MARRIAGE
TEAM US OVER TEAM ME

To our precious daughter Mallory,

You have been one of God's greatest gifts in our lives and a constant reminder of His goodness and grace. As our only child, you have brought immeasurable joy, laughter, purpose, and love into our family from the very beginning.

Watching you grow into the remarkable woman you are today has been one of our life's greatest honors. Your strength, kindness, character, and heart have blessed us more than words could ever express.

You are deeply loved, endlessly cherished, and forever treasured.

You are not only our daughter—you are now the **Rhythm of Legacy** extending from our lives.

May the faith, love, and values passed through our family continue to shine brightly through your life and through every life you impact in this world.

With all our love,
Mom and Dad

THE MARRIAGE YOU'RE BUILDING

It was year eleven.

We were sitting at the kitchen table after dinner, both of us tired, both of us distracted. Our daughter was at a friend's. The house was quiet. And somewhere in that quiet, I looked across the table at Jennsey—the woman I'd known since high school, the person I'd chosen every day for nearly two decades—and realized I wasn't sure what she was thinking. Not just that night. In general.

We weren't in crisis. We weren't fighting. We were just… orbiting each other. Two people sharing a life but not quite sharing it.

I had spent twenty years at IBM climbing through every level of corporate leadership, learning how to build systems, lead teams, and close gaps in organizations. And yet somehow the most important relationship in my life had quietly developed a gap I hadn't noticed, let alone named.

That night was the beginning of everything in this book.

Not because it was dramatic. It wasn't. But because it was honest. And honesty, we've learned, is always the first rhythm.

What you're holding is the result of what we built from that table forward—twenty-plus years of working with couples, of late-night conversations

about what actually holds a marriage together, and of learning the hard way that love alone doesn't sustain connection. Intentional rhythms do.

This is not a book about having a perfect marriage. Jennsey and I are not that couple. We are two imperfect people who have stayed, chosen, repaired, laughed, and chosen again—for more than forty years now. What we can offer you isn't a formula. It's a framework. And the difference matters.

Formulas promise results if you follow the steps. Frameworks give you a way to think so you can find your own steps. The twenty rhythms in this book are a framework—rooted in Scripture, tested in real marriages, and designed to work in the ordinary moments of your actual life.

Some of those moments are beautiful. Some are exhausting. Most are just Tuesday.

But Tuesday is where marriage is really built.

We believe there's a reason this book found its way into your hands. Not by accident—God has a purpose for you and for your marriage, and we trust He is guiding you here for something meaningful.

We won't pretend the path will always be easy. Growth asks us to be honest—not about where we wish we were, but about where we truly are. It means showing up even when it's uncomfortable. It means choosing trust and commitment even when holding back seems safer.

We invite you, as a couple, to set aside your preconceptions, take a deep breath together, and commit right now to building the marriage you truly desire. You don't need a perfect plan. You just need to stop building by accident and start building on purpose.

The very first rhythm—***The Rhythm of ONE***—is the rhythm that changes everything. It says this: **God is for you. He has good plans for you and your marriage.**

You are not alone on this journey. There is hope, purpose, and a future waiting for you both.

Forget the empty slogans about "just communicate better" or "don't forget date night." This is not another marriage book packed with vague advice and recycled formulas that leave you wondering what to do next.

This book is a blueprint for lasting connection—a collection of practical rhythms you can actually live out, not just read about. Real-world guidance for ordinary marriages facing extraordinary challenges.

You can read this alone, but it is designed to be read together. Read a chapter. Then talk about it. The questions at the end of each chapter are not optional extras—they are the most important sentences in the book.

Rooted in Scripture, this book affirms that marriage is more than a partnership—it's a covenant, an echo of God's enduring love. But it doesn't stop at inspiration. It equips you with practical tools that bridge faith and everyday action. Because *belief without practice doesn't transform*. Here, theology meets life. And real change happens.

HOW THIS BOOK IS BUILT

This book moves in two parts, and knowing the structure before you begin will help you read with intention.

Part One: Building Your Foundation (Chapters 1–8)

The first eight chapters answer the questions most couples never stop to ask: What is a rhythm, and why does it matter more than a habit? Why does drift happen even in marriages full of love? What does it mean to operate from a covenant instead of a contract? And how do you position your marriage to receive not just God's provision, but His favor?

Don't rush this section. The ground you prepare here determines how deep the next twelve chapters can take root.

Part Two: The Twelve Rhythms (Chapters 9–20)

These are the rhythms you will practice for life: Time, Communication, Friendship, Money, Adventure, Gratitude, Intimacy, Fighting Well, Forgiveness, Trust, Legacy, and the Blessing that sends you forward. Each chapter ends with conversation questions designed to be used together—not skimmed, not skipped.

If you're using the Rhythms of Marriage Companion Workbook alongside this book, each chapter corresponds directly to a workbook session with deeper tools, discussion guides, and weekly commitments. The book gives you the vision. The workbook gives you the structure to live it out.

CHAPTER 1

THE RHYTHM OF ONE

His name was David. His wife called him the hardest-working man she'd ever known, and she meant it as a compliment. He was up at five every morning, home by seven every night, leading a division of three hundred people at forty-two years old. He tithed. He coached his son's baseball team. He read his Bible on the plane between cities.

And his marriage was slowly dying.

Not loudly. Not in any way his friends would have recognized. His wife, Karen, wasn't unhappy. She was... somewhere else. She'd stopped sharing the small things—the funny thing that happened at the grocery store, the worry she had about their daughter, the quiet hope she'd been carrying for months. Not because David wouldn't listen. But because she'd learned that when he listened, he was also somewhere else.

David's problem wasn't that he didn't love God. He did. It wasn't that he didn't love Karen. He did. His problem was that his rhythm with God had become professional—efficient, consistent, and almost entirely disconnected from his heart. He read his Bible the way he read briefing documents. He prayed the way he sent emails. He worshipped on Sundays the way he attended quarterly reviews: present, prepared, and largely unreachable.

When a mentor finally asked David a simple question—"When did you last let God actually have you?"—he didn't have an answer. And in the silence that followed, something came loose.

Because here's what David had missed: you cannot give your marriage what you are not first receiving from God. You cannot offer your spouse patience you are not drawing from a source of patience. You cannot extend grace you have not first experienced. You cannot be truly present for another person when you are running on spiritual empty—no matter how disciplined your habits, how successful your career, or how good your intentions.

David's story didn't end in divorce. It ended in surrender. And then, slowly, in something better than either he or Karen had built in their first decade of marriage.

But it started with one rhythm. The first one. The one that makes all the others possible.

The Foundation God Always Intended

Every believer's life anchors on ONE relationship. When this is solid, everything aligns.

From the very beginning, God's design has always been rooted in relationship. In Genesis, we see that humanity was not created for function first, but for fellowship. God walked with Adam in the garden (Genesis 3:8), revealing that intimacy—not productivity—was the foundation of our existence. This design has never changed. We were made to know Him, to walk with Him, and to live in continual connection with Him.

Jesus makes this unmistakably clear in John 15:5: *"I am the vine; you are the branches. If you remain in me and I in you, you will bear much fruit; apart from me you can do nothing."* This isn't a suggestion—it's a defining reality. Our lives only bear lasting fruit when we stay connected to Him. Remove that connection, and everything else eventually withers.

Too often, we try to build strong marriages, lead our families well, excel in our work, and grow in influence—all without first establishing a deep, consistent rhythm with Christ. But spiritual health isn't just one part of life. It's the foundation of all life. Luke 6:48 describes a wise builder as someone who digs deep and lays the foundation on rock. When the storms come—and they will—it's the foundation that determines whether the structure stands or collapses.

But here's what happens when we don't dig deep: we build anyway. We build with whatever materials are closest, whatever seems most urgent, whatever culture tells us matters most. And for a while, it looks like it's working.

Maybe your marriage is built on career ambition—both of you hustling, climbing, providing. The house gets bigger, the titles more impressive, but the two of you grow smaller in each other's lives. Or perhaps your children have become the organizing principle. You've become co-managers of a family project rather than covenant partners walking together toward God. The kids are loved, certainly—but they were never designed to bear the weight of being your purpose.

Sometimes couples make the marriage itself the foundation, looking to each other to be their source of fulfillment, identity, spiritual anchor. When your spouse inevitably falls short, resentment creeps in—not realizing you've asked another broken human to be your savior.

Here's the painful truth: when your spiritual foundation is weak, your marriage shows it. You're physically present but emotionally distant. Conflicts escalate over small things because the real issue—spiritual emptiness—remains unaddressed. You serve each other from depletion, not overflow. Conversations stay safely on the surface because going deeper would expose how little spiritual intimacy you actually share.

Why does this happen? Because the things that replace God are often good things. Career success feeds your family. Your children need you. Your spouse does meet some of your needs. And all of it is visible, measurable, affirmed by the world around you. But time with God? That's invisible. There's no immediate catastrophe when you skip it, so it feels sustainable. You're busy, after all. Isn't a full calendar the same as a full life?

It's not. And eventually, the storm comes. The foundation is tested. And that's when you discover what you've actually been building on.

The Rhythm of ONE is about returning daily to that foundation—intentionally prioritizing time with Jesus above all else. When we're aligned with Him, our thinking and emotions stabilize, and our decisions grow wiser. Proverbs 3:5–6 reminds us: *"Trust in the Lord with all your heart and lean not on your own understanding; in all your ways submit to Him, and He will make your paths straight."*

Notice the order—trust, submit, then direction. Our relationship with God come before clarity.

God's desire for fellowship isn't distant or passive. James 4:8 says, *"Come near to God, and He will come near to you."* This is an invitation into a living, active relationship. Not a weekly check-in. Not a religious routine. A daily rhythm. A continual returning. A consistent pursuit.

When this Rhythm is right, everything else aligns. Marriages grow from fullness, not emptiness. Leadership flows from dependence on God. Purpose becomes clearer—God-directed, not self-driven.

But what does that actually look like? What changes when both of you are drawing from the same well?

Patience and grace become accessible in ways they weren't before. When you've spent the morning receiving God's mercy, you have mercy to give. You stop demanding that your spouse perform for your approval. Conflict shifts from winning to understanding. Communication deepens because vulnerability becomes possible—when your identity is secure in Christ, you don't need constant approval to feel okay. You can admit you're afraid, share the fragile dream, confess the spiritual doubt. Conversations move beyond logistics into the territory of the soul.

Conflict resolution and decision-making transform. Disagreements don't have to be won because God has already established your worth. You can actually listen, say "I was wrong," forgive from genuine release rather than gritted teeth. Career changes, financial choices, where to live—these aren't battlegrounds anymore. You're both referencing the same North Star, making decisions collaboratively and prayerfully, rooted in "What is God calling us toward?" rather than "What do I want?"

Here's the principle: when ONE is right with God, it creates a kind of spiritual gravity. Everything else gets pulled toward alignment—not through sheer effort, but through proximity to the right center. You're both orbiting the same sun. And the closer you stay to Him, the more naturally your marriage gravitates toward what He designed it to be. Toward love that's patient and kind. Toward unity that doesn't erase differences but holds them in harmony. Toward a shared purpose that's bigger than your comfort or success.

This isn't about perfection. You'll still mess up. You'll still hurt each other. But when you're both returning daily to the Rhythm of ONE, there's a gravitational pull back toward health, back toward grace, back toward each other. The marriage doesn't have to carry the weight of being your source—God does that. And from that freedom, everything else begins to flourish.

The truth is simple, but not always easy: if Jesus is not first, something else will take His place. And whatever replaces Him will never be able to sustain the weight of your life, which is why couples should always understand the devastating impact joining in a union that is not founded on God's truth.

The Rhythm we create with God always calls us back to Him—to simplicity, focus, and alignment. Here, a rhythm is not just a habit but a reliably repeated, intentionally chosen pattern of action, established and maintained in daily life, either as a couple or individually. This consistent, shared foundation shapes and sustains your connection: one relationship, one priority, one foundation.

And when that ONE is right, the things we strive for in our marriages find a gravitational pull towards the Rhythms of God.

TALK ABOUT IT

1. **If you were completely honest, what currently competes with God for first place in your life?**

    Is it your career, your children, your comfort, your phone, or even your marriage itself?

2. **What does your personal rhythm with God actually look like right now—not what you wish it looked like, but what it truly is?**

    Are you spending consistent time in prayer and Scripture, or has your spiritual life become sporadic and reactive?

3. **In what specific ways have you seen your marriage strengthen when you are spiritually healthy, and weaken when you are spiritually distant from God?**

    Can you identify patterns where your closeness to Christ directly affected your patience, grace, or ability to love your spouse well?

CHAPTER 2

THE RHYTHM OF "US"

You're in the same room. Maybe you're both scrolling on your phones, or one of you is watching TV while the other cleans up the kitchen. You might exchange a few words about tomorrow's schedule or who's picking up the kids. On the surface, everything looks fine. You're together. You're functioning. You're managing life.

But if you're honest—truly honest—you feel the distance.

You're in the same room, but you might as well be miles apart. There's no hostility, no major conflict. Just... distance. A quiet erosion of connection that happened so gradually you didn't even notice it was happening. You used to talk for hours. You used to laugh together, dream together, feel like you were building something together. Now? You're coordinating schedules. You're managing responsibilities. You're coexisting.

This is where many marriages live—not in crisis, but in drift. And here's the sobering truth: drift is just as dangerous as conflict. Maybe more so, because it's silent. It doesn't announce itself. It just slowly, quietly pulls you apart until one day you wake up next to someone who feels like a stranger.

But it doesn't have to be this way.

Marriage has a daily rhythm—a purposeful connection for unity and covenant. And when you learn to build that rhythm, everything changes. Not because your circumstances change, but because *you* change. Because the two of you, together, choose something different. Something deeper. Something worth fighting for.

From the beginning, marriage was established as the deepest human relationship. Genesis 2:24 declares, *"That is why a man leaves his father and mother and is united to his wife, and they become one flesh."* This isn't just a nice verse for wedding ceremonies. This is God's design—His blueprint for the most intimate, most vulnerable, most transformative relationship you will ever experience on this earth.

Think about what this verse is actually saying. A man leaves his father and mother—the people who gave him life, who raised him, who shaped his identity—and he is *united* to his wife. The Hebrew word for "united" here is *dabaq*, which means to cling, to adhere, to be glued together. It's not casual. It's not convenient. It's permanent, intentional, and all-consuming.

And then comes the phrase that changes everything: "they become one flesh."

This "one flesh" reality is more than physical—it is emotional, spiritual, and relational unity. It means your joys become shared joys. Your pain becomes shared pain. Your victories, your struggles, your dreams, your fears—they all belong to both of you now. No other earthly relationship is designed with this level of closeness, vulnerability, and shared identity. Not your parents. Not your children. Not your closest friends. Your spouse is meant to be the person who knows you most deeply, loves you most fully, and walks with you most intimately through every season of life.

This is what God intended. This is the vision. This is what marriage is supposed to be.

But here's the hard truth: most marriages never reach this level of unity. Not because couples don't love each other, but because they don't understand that this kind of connection requires intentionality. It requires a rhythm. It requires showing up, day after day, and choosing "us" over "me."

Many marriages drift because this rhythm is neglected. Life gets busy. Responsibilities increase. The career demands more. The kids need more. The house needs more. And somewhere in the chaos of managing it all, the marriage gets pushed to the margins. You stop asking the deep questions because you're too tired. You stop really listening because you're too distracted. You stop pursuing each other because you assume the connection will just... maintain itself.

It won't.

The truth is, strong marriages don't happen by accident. They are built through consistent investment. They are built through choosing, every single day, to prioritize your spouse. To engage emotionally. To stay curious about who they're becoming. To fight for connection even when it would be easier to just coast.

God's design calls for a marriage marked by love, sacrifice, and mutual honor. Ephesians 5:25 instructs husbands, *"Husbands, love your wives, just as Christ loved the church and gave himself up for her."*

Read that again. *"Just as Christ loved the church and gave himself up for her."*

This is not passive love. This is not "I'll love you as long as it's convenient" love. This is sacrificial, servant-hearted, intentional love. This is the kind of love that says, "I will put your needs above my own. I will serve you even when I'm tired. I will choose you even when it costs me something." This is the kind of love that doesn't wait for feelings to show up—it acts, and the feelings follow.

And here's what many people miss: this isn't just a command for husbands. Yes, husbands are called to lead in sacrificial love, but notice as Ephesians 5 continues in verse 33, it makes it clear that both husband and wife are called to mutual respect and honor. This creates a dynamic in which both spouses are pouring into one another—not keeping score, not waiting for the other person to go first, but both actively choosing to serve, to honor, to build each other up.

What does this look like on a Tuesday afternoon? It looks like this: putting down your phone when your spouse is talking to you, asking a real question and actually listening to the answer. Helping to do the dishes without being asked because you know your spouse is exhausted. Sometimes apologizing first, even when you don't think you're entirely wrong or maybe it looks like choosing kindness over being right. It all comes down to a thousand small, unglamorous choices that say, "You matter more to me than my comfort."

This rhythm requires presence. Not just physical presence, but emotional and spiritual engagement. You can be in the same room and be completely absent. You can share a bed and be emotionally disconnected. True presence means you're *there*— fully there. Your body, your mind, your heart, your attention. All of it focused on the person in front of you.

It means listening—not to respond, not to fix, not to defend yourself—but to truly understand. This shows up when asking follow-up questions or remembering what your spouse shared with you last week and checking in on it. It simply means choosing to stay connected even when it would be easier to withdraw, to shut down, or to protect yourself.

Because here's the thing: emotional withdrawal is a form of self-protection. When you've been hurt, when you're tired, when you feel misunderstood, the instinct is to pull back. To build walls. To stop trying. But every time you withdraw, you create more distance. And distance, over time, becomes the norm.

Presence is the antidote to distance. Presence says, "I'm not going anywhere. I'm staying. I'm here." And that kind of commitment—that kind of relentless, stubborn, grace-filled presence—is what transforms a marriage.

But here's the secret that changes everything: you can't do this on your own.

Ecclesiastes 4:12 reminds us, *"Though one may be overpowered, two can defend themselves. A cord of three strands is not quickly broken."* That third strand—God—binds the relationship together and gives it strength beyond what two people can sustain on their own.

This is the game-changer. This is what separates a good marriage from a God-honoring covenant. When God is at the center of your marriage, you're not just relying on your own love, your own strength, your own commitment. You're tapping into something infinitely greater. You're inviting the Creator of love Himself to be the foundation, the anchor, the source.

When both of you are pursuing God, you're naturally moving closer to each other. When both of you are seeking His wisdom, His grace, His strength, you have resources beyond yourselves to draw from. When both of you are submitting to

His design for marriage, you're building on solid ground instead of shifting sand.

God doesn't just bless your marriage from a distance. He becomes the third strand—woven into every conversation, every decision, every moment of tension, every season of joy. And that third strand makes you unbreakable. Not because you're perfect, but because He is. Not because you'll never struggle, but because He gives you what you need to persevere.

The Rhythm of US is about alignment. It is about choosing unity over individuality, connection over isolation, and covenant over convenience. It is recognizing that your spouse is not your opponent, but your partner—someone God has uniquely placed in your life to walk with you, grow with you, and build something that reflects His love.

Marriage, at its best, becomes a living picture of commitment, grace, and enduring love. That picture only comes into focus when both individuals commit to the rhythm—to showing up, to staying connected, and to building something greater than themselves.

This is a fundamental shift in perspective. In conflict, it's easy to see your spouse as the problem. As the person standing in the way of what you want. As the opponent you need to defeat in order to win the argument. But that's not God's design. God's design is partnership. It's two people, united, facing life's challenges together. It's "us against the problem," not "me against you."

When the rhythm is strong, the relationship becomes a place of strength, peace, and stability. It becomes the safe place you run to, not the place you run from. It becomes the source of joy, not just the source of obligation. It becomes the partnership that makes you better, stronger, more whole.

And in a world full of distraction and division, *The Rhythm of US* stands as a powerful testimony of what God intended marriage to be.

This is what we're building together in this book. Not a perfect marriage—those don't exist. But a strong marriage. An intentional marriage. A marriage that reflects God's design and honors the covenant you made. A marriage where you're not just coexisting, but truly connecting. Where you're not just managing life together, but building a life together.

It starts with understanding the rhythm. And it continues with choosing, every single day, to show up and build it.

TALK ABOUT IT

1. **How emotionally, spiritually, and relationally aligned do you feel with your spouse right now?**
   Are you sharing a purpose or just coexisting? Which areas are most out of sync, and why?

2. **When did you last choose unity over personal preference?**
   Recall a recent time you prioritized connection, even if it was inconvenient. How might you do this more often?

3. **Do you see your spouse as your partner or opponent?**
   During conflict, do you move closer or pull away? How does your approach reflect your beliefs about your marriage?

CHAPTER 3

HABIT -vs- RHYTHM

We often use the words "habit" and "rhythm" interchangeably when discussing our daily routines and behaviors, but there's a profound difference between these two concepts that can fundamentally change how we approach marriage. Understanding this distinction isn't just semantics, it's the key to unlocking secret melodies in marriage.

A Habit is an unconscious behavior pattern that we develop through repetition until it becomes automatic. Habits operate below the threshold of our awareness, running on autopilot in the background of our marriages. They're the things we do without thinking, without deciding, and often without even realizing we're doing them.

We know a couple who drink coffee together every morning. For the first few years, it was sacred—they sat at the kitchen table, phones away, talking about the day ahead. But somewhere along the way, it became routine. They were still sitting together, but now they scrolled through their phones, half-listening, going through the motions. The habit remained; the rhythm had died. A rhythm isn't just something you do, it's something you *protect* because you know what it creates.

When we talk about rhythms, we're not talking about grand gestures or romantic surprises. Those are nice. But they're not what sustains a marriage.

A Rhythm is a small, repeated pattern that was created intentionally.

It's the Tuesday night conversation where you actually talk—not about logistics, but about what's really happening inside you.

It's the morning coffee together before the kids wake up, where you're not solving problems, just being present.

It's the Saturday walk where you ask real questions and listen to real answers.

It's the bedtime ritual where you check in rather than scroll.

It's the way you greet each other when one of you comes home—not just a kiss, but a moment of actual attention.

These aren't romantic. They're not Instagram-worthy. But they're *powerful* because they're consistent. They're expected. They're the container in which love gets lived out, not just felt.

- Rhythm is what turns love from a feeling into practice.
- And practice is what shapes a marriage.

Question for You

Love is the foundation.

- Rhythm is the architecture.
- Architecture is what keeps the house standing.

A habit is something you do unconsciously—like automatically reaching for your phone when you sit together.

A rhythm is something you choose on purpose because it produces a result you actually want—like deciding that every evening at 8 p.m., the phones go away and you talk about your day.

A rhythm is different. It's chosen. Repeated. Protected.

It says, "We don't just hope connection happens—we make sure it happens."

- A Habit drifts.
- A Rhythm guides.

What are your current marriage habits producing right now? Distance? Tension? Disconnection? There's a pattern behind every outcome.

You don't fix your marriage by trying harder in the moment.

You change your marriage by building new rhythms that make meaningful connections your norm.

Rhythms remove the constant pressure of "When should we talk?" or "When should we reconnect?" The answer becomes simple: "We already do."

Talk with your spouse and agree to commit fully to this effort of understanding marriage rhythms and agree to take the small steps in each chapter to set your marriage on a new course—don't wait.

TALK ABOUT IT

1. **What are the current habits in our marriage— the unconscious, default patterns we fall into without thinking?**

   Be specific:

   - Do you scroll on your phone instead of talking?
   - Do you go to bed at different times?
   - Do you avoid hard conversations until they explode?
   - Do you fill every quiet moment with distractions rather than with presence?
   - Look honestly at what you're actually doing, not what you wish you were doing.
   - What patterns have become your "normal"?

2. **What are those habits producing in our marriage right now—connection or distance?**

   Think about the outcome, not the intention.

CHAPTER 4

THE DRIFT IS REAL

Lydia sits on the sofa with a book she hasn't turned a page of in twenty minutes. Mark scrolls his phone, thumb moving in that automatic rhythm that means he's not really reading anything either. The TV plays to no one. They're three feet apart.

A decade ago, they couldn't stand to be in separate rooms.

Now they share a house and live in different worlds.

No one plans this.

Nobody stands at the altar thinking, "One day we'll become polite roommates who coordinate carpool schedules and never touch."

This doesn't happen in a single fight. It happens in inches so small you don't feel them.

Remember the beginning? You stayed up until 3 AM talking about everything and nothing. You laughed so hard you couldn't breathe. You chased each other around the kitchen just to steal a kiss. You noticed the way she bit her bottom lip when she was thinking. You brought him coffee in bed on a random Tuesday because you wanted to see him smile.

You were *present* to each other.

But then life got loud.

Soccer practice every Tuesday and Thursday. Work emails at 9 PM. The baby who wouldn't sleep. The promotion that required travel. The aging parent who needed help. The second kid. The third.

One night you realize you're sitting across from each other at dinner and the only words you've said are "Can you pass the salt?" and "Did you pay the electric bill?"

You still love each other. You're still committed. You're still here.

But you're not *together*.

This slow separation—this quiet, invisible distance—is what we call **the drift**.

And it's more dangerous than any fight you'll ever have.

Because drift doesn't announce itself. There's no alarm. No breaking point. Just small patterns, repeated so often they become normal:

You say "We need to talk" and then add "but not tonight."

Date night gets canceled because you're both exhausted, and honestly, what would you even talk about?

Something bothers you, but you swallow it. "It's fine." (It's not fine.)

Your spouse is telling you about their day and you're nodding, but your eyes never leave the screen.

You say "We'll deal with it tomorrow." Tomorrow becomes next week. Next week becomes next month. Next month becomes "I don't even remember what we were upset about."

Those inches add up.

One day you look across the table and think: *How did we get here? We used to be best friends.*

Mark and Lydia aren't unique. We've sat with hundreds of couples living this exact story.

One couple didn't notice the drift until their teenage daughter asked, "Why don't you guys ever talk to each other?"

Another husband realized he felt closer to his fantasy football league than to his wife.

These weren't bad people. They weren't unloving. They were just living *reactively* instead of *intentionally*.

Maybe you see yourself in Mark and Lydia right now. Maybe you're not there yet—but you feel the pull, the drift starting. Maybe you think your marriage is strong and this doesn't apply to you. Maybe you're somewhere in between, unsure if what you're experiencing is normal or a warning sign.

Here's why we're telling you this either way: **Drift is a universal risk, not a diagnosis reserved for marriages in crisis.**

And here's the truth, whether your marriage is in crisis, sensing danger, or seems fine on the surface:

You are not as strong as you think without intentionality.

None of us are.

"Pretty good" is the most dangerous place a marriage can be.

Because "pretty good" doesn't force you to change. It doesn't create urgency. It lets you coast.

And coasting always leads backward.

Marriages don't usually explode. They erode. They become comfortable, predictable, unchallenged. You stop fighting for each other because there's nothing dramatic to fight against.

And what you don't fight for, you slowly lose.

You don't drift into a better marriage.

You drift away from one.

This book exists to show you something critical: **Your daily routines—not your good intentions—determine the strength of your marriage.**

You can *want* closeness. You can *value* your spouse. You can *believe* in your commitment.

But if your daily patterns don't reflect those values, they don't matter.

Because if you don't choose your rhythms, you will inherit them.

And inherited rhythms—the ones you fall into by default—rarely build the marriage you want.

So let's stop drifting.

Let's recognize what's happening and choose a different direction.

Starting today.

Whether you're in crisis recognizing the damage, catching warning signs early, or trying to prevent something before it starts—what comes next is for you. Real change doesn't require your marriage to be broken. It requires intention. And intention looks the same whether you're rebuilding from distance or protecting against it. The work ahead isn't about your marriage's current state. It's about choosing to be deliberate instead of reactive, starting now.

What Real Change Actually Looks Like

We need to tell you something that might disappoint you:

Change doesn't happen in one conversation.

It doesn't happen in one week.

It doesn't even happen in one month.

Real change happens through repeated, imperfect attempts over time.

Your First Attempts Will Feel Clumsy

And that's not a sign you're doing it wrong.

That's a sign you're doing it *right*.

When you sit down with your spouse and try to have a real conversation after months—or years—of surface-level talk, it's going to feel awkward. You might not know what to say. You might deflect with a joke. You might get defensive. You might cry. You might just sit there in silence, staring at your hands.

All of that is normal.

All of that is part of the process.

The couples we've worked with who actually transformed their marriages weren't the ones who got it right the first time.

They were the ones who got it wrong, acknowledged it, and tried again.

But here's the warning we want to give you:

Awareness without action becomes regret.

You can know your marriage is drifting. You can see the problem clearly. And you can still choose to do nothing about it.

You can decide it's too hard. Too awkward. Too uncertain.

And for a while, that might feel easier.

But regret is heavier than awkwardness.

Regret is what you carry when you look back five years from now and realize you *could* have done something. You saw it happening. You knew. And you chose silence anyway.

So we're asking you: **Choose the awkwardness.**

Choose the imperfect conversation.

Choose to show up, even when you don't know what you're doing.

Because a clumsy attempt at connection is infinitely more valuable than a perfect silence.

Your marriage isn't waiting for you to be ready.

It's waiting for you to begin.

TALK ABOUT IT

1. **Drift can threaten any marriage, even those that seem strong or comfortable.**
   It's not just couples in crisis who are at risk; every relationship needs attention and intentionality to avoid drifting apart. Vigilance is essential for lasting marriages.

2. **Where do you notice drift or feel most vulnerable?**
   Often, it's the small things: missed conversations, delayed quality time, faded jokes, or routine affection. Consider where you've become more like roommates than partners.

3. **What fears arise when thinking about change?**
   We may hesitate due to concerns about failure, awkwardness, or disrupting comfort. Identify your underlying fears and ask what it would take to act despite them.

CHAPTER 5

NOT GETTING THERE BY ACCIDENT

There is a real gap between knowing and doing.

Knowing the drift is real is one thing, but doing something proactive doesn't accidentally happen.

Most couples don't intend for that gap to grow.

But it can. And it does without being intentional.

The dishwasher hummed. Mark's thumb scrolled—blue light washing over his face in the dim kitchen. Janet's hands moved through warm, soapy water, loading plates one by one.

Tuesday night. Nothing special.

Nothing broken, really.

But something was missing.

And Janet finally named it.

"I thought marriage would be different."

Her voice was quiet. Steady. Not angry. Not accusatory.

Just honest.

"This isn't what I expected."

Mark's thumb stopped mid-scroll. Every nerve ending screamed *defend yourself*—but he didn't. He looked up. He listened.

"I thought we'd feel more... connected," Janet said, not looking at him. "I thought we'd know each other better by now. I thought marriage would feel easier than this."

The silence between them stretched.

And there it was.

The gap.

When Mark and Janet got married, they had a vision.

They could both see it clearly—a marriage full of laughter and deep conversation. They'd understand each other intuitively. Intimacy would be natural, effortless. Date nights would feel spontaneous and meaningful. They'd be each other's best friends.

Love would sustain all of that.

But what they didn't have was a system.

Mark and Janet had a vision.

They had no structure.

Love alone doesn't sustain vision. Love gives you the *reason* to build something.

But rhythms give you a *way* to build it.

So what did they do?

At first, they tried harder at the wrong things.

Mark thought the problem was romance. So he planned elaborate date nights—expensive restaurants he couldn't afford, coordinated schedules that required military precision, manufactured "spontaneity" that felt exhausting and performative. He'd light candles. He'd queue up playlists. He'd try to recreate something that felt increasingly out of reach.

Janet thought the problem was her. She wasn't interesting enough. Wasn't available enough. So she stayed up late when she was exhausted, pretending to have energy she didn't have. She said yes when she meant no. She tried to be more of whatever she thought he wanted.

Both worked harder.

In the wrong direction.

And the blame crept in—subtle, unspoken.

If you were more present, I'd feel more connected.

If you weren't so stressed about work, we could actually enjoy each other.

They were treating symptoms.

Not the cause.

The cause was this: their marriage dreams had no design.

Marriage is like a boat on a current.

Picture it: you're in a small boat, and the water is always moving. Always pulling. The current doesn't care about your intentions or your love or your history.

It just moves.

Every day, you're either rowing toward each other or drifting apart.

There is no neutral.

Some couples seem effortless—they laugh easily, finish each other's sentences, protect their time, align around values, keep life adventurous. You watch them and think: *They're lucky.*

But it's not luck.

It's built rhythms.

They're rowing. Not flawlessly. Not perfectly. But consistently.

Their hands are on the oars. They feel the resistance of the water. They pull. They adjust. They pull again.

And slowly—stroke by stroke—they move toward each other.

Drifting looks different. Drifting is passive. You're still in the boat together, but your hands aren't on the oars. The current pulls you sideways. Then backward. You look up one day and realize you can barely see each other across the distance.

Consistency is what builds strength.

Not intensity. Not perfection.

Consistency.

You don't need a perfect marriage.

You need purposeful patterns to shape your marriage.

The Turning Point

The shift came when Mark and Janet stopped asking the wrong question.

"Why don't we feel connected?" didn't lead anywhere.

So they asked a different one: "What would actually *create* connection?"

Not romance. Not grand gestures.

Small, repeated patterns they both consistently showed up for.

They started with Tuesday nights. Fifteen minutes. Phones off. Not talking about schedules or logistics—talking about what was actually happening in their hearts.

The first Tuesday, Mark expected it to fail. He thought Janet would say she was too tired, or he'd run out of things to say. But she showed up. And he did too.

They talked about work stress. About feeling distant. About missing each other even though they lived in the same house.

It wasn't magic. But it was real.

Then Saturday mornings. A walk together, even if it was just around the block. The first Saturday, they barely talked—just walked side by side, breathing the same air. But by the third Saturday, something had shifted. They were laughing again.

A moment before bed where they checked in instead of collapsing into sleep.

Nothing fancy. Nothing that required perfect conditions.

Just rhythms.

And here's what they discovered: the vision didn't change. Mark and Janet still wanted that amazing marriage they dreamed about from the beginning.

But the path to it wasn't through trying harder or just being better.

It was through building small intentional efforts, so connection became inevitable instead of accidental.

So when you look at the gap between what you expected and what you're experiencing—

Don't see it as a failure.

See it as information.

The feelings arising from your unmet expectations aren't telling you that you chose the wrong person or that your marriage is broken. Those feelings tell you something much more useful.

They tell you: *"This is what matters. And this is what needs to be built."*

If you expected to feel known and you don't, that's information. It means you need rhythms of deeper conversation.

If you expected to feel desired and you don't, that's information. It means you need to intentionally rebuild emotional and physical intimacy.

If you expected to feel like a team and you don't, that's information. It means you need to align on values and vision.

Your unmet expectations are a map.

They're showing you exactly where to build.

And the beautiful thing is this: the marriage you dreamed about isn't lost.

It's just waiting to be constructed.

Not by accident, But on purpose.

We redefine what we're building.

Not based on what we imagine.

But based on:

- What actually works
- What actually lasts
- What actually builds connection

Because the goal isn't to recreate a dream.

It's to build something real.

Something:

- Tested
- Intentional
- Sustainable

This requires letting go of unrealistic expectations, so you can embrace intentional construction.

The marriage you dreamed about will only become real when you build it on purpose.

Scripture says, "Trust in the Lord and do good" (Psalm 37:3).

Not just trust. Act.

Most couples trust God with their marriage but don't take responsibility for building it. They pray for connection yet don't make time for it. They want intimacy but avoid the hard conversations that lead to it. They desire growth but resist the changes it requires.

A thriving marriage doesn't just happen by chance.

It is designed and built on purpose.

Whether you realize it or not, your current rhythms are already producing your current marriage.

If something appears wrong...

If something appears missing...

If something appears stuck...

That's information. That's design work waiting to be done.

Mark and Janet eventually chose a different path. They gave their struggles to God, leaned on His Word, and started building new rhythms. What felt like the end became the start of a restored marriage centered on Christ.

Love was still there—but now it had structure.

TALK ABOUT IT

1. **What's the gap between your ideal marriage and your current reality?**
   Focus on the small things—connection, time together, easy conversation.

2. **What do unmet expectations reveal?**
   See them as clues.

3. **What's one step to move closer to the marriage you want?**
   Choose a simple, regular habit—like a weekly check-in or walk—to reconnect and rebuild what's missing.

CHAPTER 6

LET'S MEET FUTURE US

Close your eyes for a moment and imagine this:

You're walking into your living room twenty years from now. Your spouse is sitting in their favorite chair. You catch their eye, and they smile—the kind of smile that carries decades of inside jokes, weathered storms, and chosen faithfulness.

What does the air between you feel like?

Is it warm? Easy? The kind of comfort that comes from two people who've built something real together—who know each other's stories, finish each other's sentences, and still choose each other on the hard days?

Or is it... polite? Distant? Like two people who share a mortgage and a last name but not much else? The kind of distance where you can be in the same room and still feel completely alone?

Here's the uncomfortable truth: most couples never have this conversation.

They talk about what's for dinner. They coordinate schedules and discuss the kids' activities. They debate whether to refinance the house or where to go on vacation. But they rarely—if ever—sit down and ask the question that matters most:

Who are we becoming?

Because here's what we've learned after years of working with couples: your marriage is moving in a direction right now. Every single day, you're building something—whether you realize it or not.

The danger isn't that you'll wake up one morning and suddenly be in a terrible marriage. The danger is that you'll wake up one morning in a marriage you never intended to build—one that happened by default and drift instead of by design.

Think about it.

You come home exhausted after a long day. Your spouse is tired, too. You both collapse on the couch, pull out your phones, and scroll in silence for an hour before bed. It feels justified in the moment—you're tired, you need to decompress, you'll connect tomorrow.

But tomorrow, you're tired again. And the next day. And the next.

Six months later, you realize you can't remember the last time you had a real conversation. A year later, you're living like roommates. Five years later, you're wondering how you got here.

That's how it happens. Not in one catastrophic moment, but in a thousand small choices that felt reasonable at the time.

Or picture this: You're frustrated about the same issue again—maybe it's how your spouse handles conflict, or their relationship with their phone, or the way they parent differently than you do. You've brought it up before, and it didn't go well. So this time, you just... don't. You swallow it. You tell yourself it's not worth the fight.

But the frustration doesn't disappear. It just goes underground. And next time, you swallow it again. And again. Until one day, you realize you've built a wall between you—brick by brick, silence by silence—and you don't even know how to talk to each other anymore.

These aren't dramatic failures. They're just... life. Tiredness. Busyness. Conflict avoidance. The path of least resistance.

But here's what most couples don't realize: **the path of least resistance doesn't lead to a neutral place. It leads somewhere specific. And it's probably not where you want to go.**

We know a couple—let's call them Daniel and Mia—who hit this wall after fifteen years of marriage. They weren't fighting. They weren't in crisis. They were just... existing. Going through the motions. Checking boxes.

One night, Mia looked at Daniel across the dinner table and asked a question that changed everything:

"If nothing changes in the next ten years—if we keep doing exactly what we're doing right now—where will we be?"

Daniel opened his mouth to answer, then stopped. Because the honest answer scared him.

They'd be further apart. More distant. More like strangers. They'd have raised their kids, paid off the house, and built successful careers—but they'd have lost each other in the process.

That fear became fuel.

They realized they'd been making decisions based on how they felt *today*—tired, overwhelmed, stretched thin—instead of who they wanted to be *tomorrow*. And those daily choices were writing a story they didn't want to live.

So they made a different choice.

Not a dramatic one. Not a complete life overhaul. Just one small decision: they committed to fifteen minutes of conversation every night before bed. No phones. No TV. Just the two of them, talking about something real.

It felt awkward at first. Forced, even. But they kept showing up. And slowly—so slowly they almost didn't notice— something shifted. It wasn't magic. They still had terrible days. They still got frustrated and tired. But they kept showing up. And that consistency—more than any single conversation or perfect evening—was what changed everything. The distance started to close. The warmth started to return. They started remembering why they chose each other in the first place.

That's the power of "Future Us" thinking.

Before you can design the marriage you want, you have to face the marriage you have—with complete, unflinching honesty.

Not the version you present to friends or post on social media, and not the version you tell yourself when you're feeling defensive.

The real version.

Where are you actually right now?

Maybe you're like Daniel and Mia—not in crisis, but not really connected either. You love each other, but you're not *close*. You share a life, but you don't share your hearts.

You might be exhausted—drowning in work and kids and responsibilities—and your marriage is getting whatever's left over at the end of the day. Which is usually nothing.

You may even feel stuck in the same arguments, the same patterns, the same frustrations you've been cycling through for years. And you're starting to wonder if this is just how it's going to be.

Or you may be those few couples reading this and thinking, "We're actually doing okay." And you are. But "okay" isn't the same as thriving. And you know—deep down—that there's more available to you than just "fine."

Here's what we've learned: **there's always a gap between the marriage you want and the marriage you're actually living.**

That gap isn't a judgment. It's just reality. Because life is hard, and marriage is harder, and none of us are doing this perfectly.

But here's the hope: **that gap can be closed. One decision at a time.**

Not through feelings. Not through hoping things get better. Not through waiting for your spouse to change first.

Through decisions.

Small, daily, repeated decisions that move you toward "Future Us" instead of away from it.

- The decision to put your phone down when your spouse is talking.
- The decision to have the hard conversation rather than avoid it.
- The decision to protect your time together, even when you're tired.
- The decision to say "I'm sorry" instead of "I'm right."
- The decision to choose connection over comfort, vulnerability over self-protection, and intentionality over drift.

These decisions don't feel life-changing in the moment. But they compound. Day after day, week after week, year after year—they build the marriage you're going to live in twenty years from now.

Your daily patterns are writing your future. Right now. Whether you're paying attention or not.

The question isn't whether you're building something. You are. The question is: **Are you building what you actually want?**

If that question makes you uncomfortable, good. That discomfort is the beginning of change.

Because the truth is, most of us are building by accident. We're reacting to how we feel today instead of designing for who we want to be tomorrow. We're letting life happen to us instead of making intentional choices about the life—and the marriage—we're creating.

But it doesn't have to be that way.

You can choose differently. Starting today.

Not perfectly. Not all at once. Just one decision at a time.

Daniel and Mia's story didn't end with that one conversation. It started there. They still have hard days. They still get tired, frustrated, and overwhelmed. But now, when they're faced with a choice—scroll on their phones or talk to each other, avoid the conflict or lean into it, let another week slip by or protect their time together—they ask themselves:

"Does this decision move us toward Future Us or away from it?"

And then they choose accordingly.

That's the shift. That's the power of vision, meeting honesty, meeting intentionality.

You don't need to have it all figured out. You don't need a perfect plan. You just need to stop building by accident and start building on purpose.

The marriage you want twenty years from now is being decided right now—in this moment, in today's choices, in the rhythms you're building or neglecting.

So let's get honest. Let's get intentional. Let's close the gap between "Current Us" and "Future Us."

Not someday. Not when life calms down. Not when you feel more motivated.

Now.

Because your marriage is worth it. Your spouse is worth it. And the life you could build together—the warmth, the closeness, the deep, easy familiarity that comes from decades of chosen faithfulness—is absolutely worth fighting for.

The question is: are you willing to start building it today?

TALK ABOUT IT

1. **Picture your marriage twenty years from now—not the house, kids, or other external stuff.**

   Describe the marriage itself. What does an average day look like? How do you talk, laugh, and handle hard things?

2. **Now look at Current Us with complete honesty.**

   Where are you right now—just the truth of today? How much time do you protect for each other, and how much gets swallowed by busyness?

3. **What one small daily choice is moving you away from Future Us?**

   Not the big stuff—the small, repeated choice you make on autopilot.

CHAPTER 7

CONTRACT -vs- COVENANT

On average, marriages don't fail because love runs out.

They struggle because of a destructive agreement they try to live under.

On paper, you're married. Underneath, you're operating from either a contract or a covenant.

- A Contract is built on lack of trust, which is why we have so many legal documents for everything. In our humanity, we don't naturally trust, we are skeptical.

- A Covenant is built completely on trust. This trust comes because the trust is in God. In a marriage covenant God is part of it. He is the reason we can trust—because He will never let us down even when the couple does.

Allow me to show you what that looks like when the rubber meets the road.

The Contract Marriage – Jessica and Tyler

Jessica and Tyler had been married fourteen years when the contract became unavoidable to ignore.

It commenced small, the way these things usually do. Tyler would come home from a long day at the office, kick off his shoes, and collapse on the couch with his phone. Jessica, who had already cooked dinner, helped the kids with homework, shuttled them to practices, and folded three loads of laundry, would feel the usual burn rise in her torso.

I did all this today, she thought. The least he could do is notice me. Thank me. Help me.

So she started keeping score—silently at first.

If he forgot to text her during the day, she gave him the cold shoulder that night.

If he didn't initiate sex or romance, she emotionally withdrew for days.

If he left dishes in the sink again, she let resentment simmer until it boiled over in a sharp, sarcastic remark: "Must be nice to have a personal maid who never gets a day off."

Tyler kept his own quiet tally on the other side of the wall they were building.

She never appreciates the overtime I work so we can afford this house and these vacations.

She criticizes how I discipline the kids, but never steps up when I'm exhausted from providing.

She needs me to be more affectionate, but she's always too tired, too mad, or too checked out.

Their affection hadn't died. They still cared deeply in moments. But everything had become conditional: "I will… if you do."

Patience only if respect was shown first.

Affection only if needs were met first.

Forgiveness only if the apology sounded perfect and came with flowers.

They were both exhausted from the negotiation table, which they never agreed to sit at. Arguments ended with one of them storming off, muttering, "Fine. I'll just do it myself." Intimacy seemed like a transaction that required perfect performance. Trust declined because deep down, both were asking the same fearful question: If I mess up one more time, will they finally pull away for good?

That's a contract marriage.

It seems fair and balanced—until it slowly suffocates everything beautiful that once drew you together.

The Covenant Marriage – Ben and Rachel

Now meet Ben and Rachel.

Three years into their marriage, Rachel was diagnosed with an aggressive form of breast cancer. The lively, adventurous woman Ben had married—the one who took him on spontaneous hikes, made him laugh until his sides hurt, and brightened every room—suddenly became frail, lost her hair from chemo, and was kept awake at night by fear.

In a contract marriage, this would have been the breaking point. Ben could have kept score: I'm already working full-time, managing the kids' schedules, paying the mounting medical bills, and now I'm also the full-time caretaker? When do I get my needs met? When is it my turn?

Instead, Ben chose covenant.

Every morning before leaving for work, he sat upon the edge of their bed, took her cold hand in his, and prayed Psalm 23 over her with a steady voice: "The Lord is my shepherd; I shall not want... Even though I walk through the valley of the shadow of death, I will fear no evil, for You are with me." Even on the mornings she was too nauseous or angry to respond, he stayed. He learned to cook the few bland foods her stomach could handle. He shaved his own head in solidarity so she wouldn't feel alone in her baldness. When the pain made her push him away and snap in frustration, he didn't retreat or retaliate. He moved in closer, choosing gentleness when each instinct cried out for self-protection.

One particularly dark night, after a brutal round of chemo left her weak and weeping, Rachel said through tears, "I feel like I'm ruining your life. You didn't sign up for this."

Ben looked her straight in the eyes, brushed a tear from her cheek, and whispered firmly, "You're not ruining anything. I didn't marry the healthy, energetic version of you. I married you—all of you. And I'm choosing you today, tomorrow, and every hard day after that. Not because you can give me something back right now. But because I was before God and said 'I do' to all of you, in sickness and in health, for better or worse. I'm not keeping score. I'm keeping my promise."

That moment didn't miraculously erase the cancer or the pain. But it rebuilt something even deeper than romance ever could. It rebuilt rock-solid trust.

Rachel later shared, "In the middle of the worst season of my life, I never once wondered if Ben would leave or resent me. That safety gave me courage—not just to fight the cancer, but to fight for our marriage. It reminded me that I wasn't a burden; I was still his chosen one."

Ben wasn't playing the hero. He was simply living what God designed marriage to be: a covenant.

A Second Story of Covenant in the Fire – Gary and Lisa

Years after their wedding, Gary and Lisa's marriage hit rock bottom. Gary had an affair. The betrayal shattered Lisa. She felt humiliated, angry, and totally alone. Friends told her she had every right to walk away. In a contract mindset, the marriage would have ended right there—"You broke the deal; I'm out."

But Lisa chose a different path. She turned to God in her pain, spending hours in her walk-in closet on her knees, lights off, tears flowing, confessing her own shortcomings in the marriage and asking Him to heal her heart first. She called her pastor late one night and admitted everything—the anger, the shame, the temptation to leave. He connected her with a Christian counselor who specialized in infidelity, and Lisa began writing honest, humble letters—first to family, then to Gary—owning her part without excusing his.

Gary was stunned by her response. Instead of the retaliation he expected, he saw a wife who refused to let betrayal define their story. Over months of hard, honest conversations, counseling, and prayer, Gary repented deeply. He chose to fight for the marriage with the same intentionality Lisa showed.

One common afternoon at a flea market—far from any romantic setting—Gary kissed her cheek, they hugged, and something changed. The covenant they had made before God proved stronger than the worst mistake either had made. Today, years later, they describe their marriage as restored and even sweeter, a living testimony that covenant love can bring resurrection after death looks certain.

God's Design for a Covenant Marriage

Scripture is crystal clear. God doesn't describe marriage as a business deal or temporary agreement. In Malachi 2:14, He calls the wife "your partner, the wife of your marriage covenant." In Ephesians 5:31-32, Paul reveals the deep mystery: marriage is a living picture of Christ's unbreakable covenant love for His bride, the church. Jesus didn't love us because we performed perfectly—He loved us while we were still sinners and gave Himself up for us anyway (Romans 5:8).

Covenant love isn't about always getting something in return or only loving your spouse when they deserve it. Instead, it's about showing up with steady commitment—even on hard days, even when you don't feel like it, even when your spouse can't give much back. This kind of love means keeping your promises and choosing to act with kindness, even when life gets tough or your emotions are all over the place. It's like deciding every day: I'll love you not because you've earned it, but because I promised I would.

Imagine a time when your spouse was discouraged, sick, or struggling, and couldn't give you much attention in return. Covenant love is what keeps you bringing them a cup of tea, offering a gentle touch, or saying, "I'm here," even when you feel tired or frustrated. You do it not because you always feel a rush of love, but because you're honoring the commitment you made. This is the heart of the scriptural model of unconditional love—loving on purpose, no matter what.

Covenant feels risky—you're leading with love without a guarantee of instant return. But here's what most couples miss: covenant doesn't create weakness. It creates unbreakable safety and stability.

When both people operate this way, trust skyrockets. You stop wondering, "Will they pull away if I mess up?" You know where you stand. The relationship is no longer fragile because it's anchored within something way stronger than feelings or circumstances.

Most couples drift into contract because it seems natural and self-protective—"I'll do my part if you do yours." Covenant is always intentional.

So here's the question that matters more than any other in this chapter:

How are you actually showing up when expectations aren't met?

- Do you withdraw when your spouse doesn't meet your needs?
- Do you give conditionally?
- Do you keep mental records of every shortcoming?

Or…

- Do you stay engaged anyway?
- Do you choose consistency instead of convenience?
- Do you act with commitment, even when it costs you?

Your framework determines your future.

Rhythms built on a conditional contract will always crack under pressure.

Rhythms built on covenant? They endure—because they're anchored in the same promise God made to us: "I will never leave you nor forsake you" (Hebrews 13:5).

Ben and Rachel walked through cancer and came out stronger. Gary and Lisa walked through betrayal and found restoration. Their marriages didn't survive because life suddenly got easier. They survived—and thrived—because they chose covenant when everything in them wanted to choose self-protection.

You have the same choice—today, during the small moments no one sees: the eye-roll you swallow, the grace you extend when you're tired, the decision to stay engaged instead of shutting down.

Will you keep score... or keep your promise?

The answer is quietly writing the next chapter of your marriage right now.

1. **Are you keeping score or keeping promises in your marriage?** When your spouse disappoints you, what's your first instinct?

2. **Does your spouse feel safe being honest with you?** Or do they feel like they're being evaluated?

3. **When expectations aren't met, will you withdraw—or stay engaged?** That's the covenant question.

CHAPTER 8

BLESSING -vs- FAVOR

You can have God's blessing on your marriage and still miss His favor.

And most couples don't even know there's a difference.

They pray for a breakthrough. They ask God to "fix" their relationship. They want the intimacy, the unity, the joy they see in other marriages. But nothing changes. And they wonder why God isn't showing up.

Here's the truth many couples miss: **Marriage isn't only relational. It's deeply spiritual.** And you can't fix spiritual brokenness with purely relational effort.

There's a distinction that changes everything—one that determines whether your marriage simply survives under God's provision or actually *thrives* under His favor.

Blessing is what God gives His children simply because they belong to Him. It's His daily provision— protection, provision, peace. Just like a good father provides food, shelter, and care for his children because they're his, God blesses us because we are His. We don't earn it. We don't deserve it. It flows from His nature as Father.

"And God is able to bless you abundantly, so that in all things at all times, having all that you need, you will abound in every good work" (2 Corinthians 9:8).

Favor, on the other hand, is what God pours out when we align our lives with His will. It's the special smile of God—His delight, His approval, His supernatural empowerment. Favor isn't automatic. It's responsive. It comes when we move toward Him and order our lives according to His design.

"Let the favor of the Lord our God be upon us, and establish the work of our hands" (Psalm 90:17).

Let me show you what this looks like.

I remember one afternoon when my daughter and I went to the park for lunch. She was just seven years old. We picked up sandwiches and sat down to watch the squirrels. While we were eating, my daughter noticed a homeless man sitting alone on a bench nearby.

"Daddy, who is that?" she asked.

I told her he was someone who didn't have a home.

Without hesitation, she picked up her bag, walked straight over to him, and said, "Hey, Mister, are you hungry?" She held out her sandwich. He took it, surprised, and started eating. Then she ran back, grabbed her drink, and brought it to him, too.

At that moment, my heart swelled. My daughter delighted everything inside me. She didn't do it because I told her to. She did it because compassion moved her.

Now, here's the thing: my daughter didn't always obey me. There were plenty of days she tested boundaries, talked back, or ignored what I asked her to do. But even in her disobedience, she never fell out of my *blessing*. I still fed her. I still clothed her. I still tucked her in at night. Because she was mine.

But *favor*? That's different. Favor is what I gave her out of delight. When she was disobedient, she still got dinner—but she didn't get a trip to the toy store. She still had a bed to sleep in—but she didn't get ice cream after dinner.

Blessing sustained her. Favor rewarded her alignment with my heart.

That's not just a parenting principle—that's a kingdom principle. And it works exactly the same way in your marriage.

And this is exactly how it works in marriage.

Too many couples sit back, waiting for God to "fix" their relationship while remaining passive. They pray for harmony but aren't actively becoming more patient. They ask for intimacy but don't protect time together. They want unity but refuse to submit their individual preferences to God's design for marriage.

They live under God's blessing—He still provides, He still sustains—but they wonder why breakthrough never comes. Why do their prayers feel unanswered? Why do other couples seem to experience something they can't access?

To understand how couples move from blessing to favor in marriage, we have to understand how spiritual leadership works in God's design—not as control, but as flow.

The answer, in part, comes down to how spiritual leadership works in God's design for marriage—and this may be where some readers need to pause. This isn't a detour into theology for its own sake. It's the most practical thing in this chapter, because what flows through the spiritual leader of a home either nourishes or depletes everything under that covering. To understand how favor moves, we need to see what Scripture shows us about how spiritual weight works.

Spiritual Leadership Designed for Spiritual Flow

There are clear pictures presented in the Bible of how God's blessings and favor flow as well as the structure He has put into place for "men", as they fulfill their spiritual roles as spiritual leaders.

In Joshua 7 there is a story of a man named Achan. Achan was an Israelite who fought the battle of Jericho with Joshua. God had commanded the Israelites to destroy the entire city of Jericho because of its great sin.

Only Rahab the harlot and her household were spared because she had hidden the Israelite spies. God further commanded that, unlike most victories when soldiers were allowed to take the spoils, the Israelites were to take nothing from Jericho.

Everything in it was "devoted to destruction." God warned that anyone taking spoils from Jericho would "make the camp of Israel liable to destruction and bring trouble on it". The Israelites obeyed, except for Achan, who stole a beautiful robe and some gold and silver and hid these things in his tent.

His sin was discovered, of course. God commanded that Achan and his entire family and all his possessions be destroyed. Achan's sin affected the entire nation of Israel. In Joshua 7:1 God says that "the Israelites" acted unfaithfully and that His anger burned "against Israel."

The nation as a whole was in a covenant relationship with God and, when one member transgressed that covenant, the entire nation's relationship with Him was damaged. Achan's sin defiled the other members of the community as well as himself.

A similar situation is seen in the sin of Adam and Eve and its effect on the whole of mankind. Adam and Eve's rebellion destroyed the perfect communion the human race would have enjoyed with God.

This is a sobering reality: the choices of a spiritual leader carry weight far beyond themselves. What Achan did in secret didn't just affect him—it brought consequences on everyone under his covering. That principle hasn't changed. But here's the good news: we live under grace now, and the punishment for sin doesn't fall directly on us because Jesus has already paid that price.

The structure of a man's role as spiritual leader hasn't changed. Today the spiritual leader still provides and protects, but there is a bigger responsibility in play, especially when it comes to the family.

Everything that was under the leadership of Achan received the same punishment, because it was under his covering of accountability. The spiritual leader today sits in the role as more of a funnel than an umbrella.

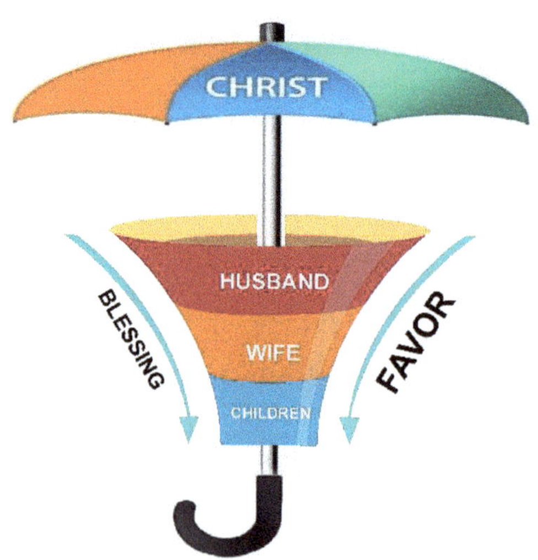

Jesus is the umbrella. He covers and protects. The spiritual leader of the home now serves to disperse the spiritual gifts from heaven to his spouse and family.

What does that look like? It means he prays for his wife and children's spiritual growth. It means he makes decisions with their hearts and souls in mind, not just their schedules. It means he creates space in the home for God to work—through his words, his example, his leadership—and gently guides his family toward Christ, not through control, but through love that reflects Jesus.

Christian Couples Usually Live in Blessing but Miss Favor

I know a couple—let's call them Daniel and Sarah—who prayed for years that God would "restore the spark" in their marriage. They went to church. They tithed. They loved Jesus. But their marriage felt flat. Distant. They were roommates more than lovers.

One day, a mentor asked them a hard question: "Are you actually *doing* what God's Word says about marriage? Are you serving each other? Pursuing each other? Protecting your time together? Speaking life over one another?"

The answer was no. They were waiting for God to move while ignoring the clear instructions He'd already given.

When they finally aligned their marriage with Scripture—when the husband began leading with sacrificial love, the wife responded with respect and support, and they prioritized weekly time together and chose vulnerability over self-protection—everything shifted. Not because God suddenly decided to bless them, but because they stepped into the place where His *favor* could flow.

Here's the truth: God's design for marriage isn't arbitrary. When husbands love their wives as Christ loved the church—sacrificially, consistently, with servant leadership—and when wives honor and support their husbands with grace and strength, something supernatural happens. Not because you've earned it, but because you've aligned with the way God built marriage to work.

Biblical leadership isn't about control. Biblical submission isn't about weakness. Both are about mutual honor, both rooted in love, both reflecting the relationship between Christ and the church. And when you live that out—when you stop waiting and start building—you position your marriage to receive not just God's provision, but His *favor*.

So here's the question:

Are you living under a blessing, passively waiting for God to fix what you're unwilling to align with?

Or are you actively bringing your marriage into alignment with His will—protecting time, speaking life, serving sacrificially, pursuing intentionally—and positioning yourself to experience His favor?

Because God is ready to pour out more than you can imagine. But favor doesn't come to those who wait. It comes to those who obey.

TALK ABOUT IT

1. **Are we waiting for God to fix our marriage, or are we actively making changes?**
   Where are you asking for breakthrough but not taking practical steps—like prioritizing time together, communicating honestly, or creating a budget?

2. **What does real alignment with God's design look like in your marriage this week?**
   Instead of staying theoretical, identify what it means to love sacrificially, speak positively, serve when tired, and commit even when unmotivated.

3. **Are we seeking God's blessing while remaining passive?**
   Consider where you want God to intervene without facing the issues yourself or changing your own behavior. God's favor calls for partnership; what active step will you take this week?

CHAPTER 9

THE RHYTHM OF TIME

Most couples don't protect their marriage because they don't see time together as sacred. They see it as a luxury—something to fit in after kids, work, and obligations are taken care of. And so it's the first thing to suffer.

You don't lose connection in one dramatic explosion. You lose it in quiet minutes that slip away unnoticed.

A conversation you skipped because the kids needed help with homework. A moment you were half-present, scrolling your phone instead of truly seeing your spouse. A night you chose work emails or another episode over sitting close on the couch. A week consumed entirely by "too busy" until another month disappeared without a trace.

Those small, repeated choices stack up like unseen dust until, on a typical evening, you look across the room and think, *When did we stop feeling close?* Not because of a big betrayal, but because nothing intentional took its place.

Take Alex and Bre, a young couple just a few years into marriage with two toddlers in diapers. Their days had moved from romance to pure survival: cook, feed, clean, change diapers, work, collapse into bed, repeat. By 10 p.m. most nights, they were exhausted shells of themselves. Conversations had shrunk to bare logistics—"Did you buy milk?"

Touch had become rare and functional. They still loved each other deeply, but the electric spark that once kept them talking and laughing until 2 a.m. had quietly waned into shared space without shared hearts.

They weren't fighting. They were simply drifting in the current of a busy season—exactly the kind of drift the Song of Solomon warns against.

Here's the truth that cuts straight through the noise of contemporary life:

Healthy marriages need to be constantly fed and nurtured through spending regular, intentional time together.

That's not a civil suggestion. It's a living, breathing biblical reality, beautifully painted in the Song of Solomon—God's passionate poem celebrating covenant love.

In Song of Solomon 2:10-13, the lover calls to his beloved with urgent delight:

"Arise, my love, my beautiful one, and come away. For behold, the winter is past; the rain is over and gone. The flowers appear on the earth; the time of singing has come…"

Twice, he invites her—"Arise… and come away." He doesn't wait for a perfect, convenient moment. He intentionally draws her out of the ordinary rhythm of life into a season of beauty, singing, fragrance, and closeness. The winter of emotional distance doesn't have to last. The season of singing can return—if you choose to respond to the invitation.

This pursuit isn't one-sided. The bride echoes the longing in Song of Solomon 8:14: "Make haste, my beloved, and be like a gazelle or a young stag on the mountains of spices." She eagerly looks forward to time with him, no matter where he is or what he's doing. And at times of separation or tiredness, she shows unceasing pursuit: "I sought him whom my soul loves… I will rise now and go about the city… I found him whom my soul loves. I held him and would not let him go" (Song of Solomon 3:1-4).

Love in the Song doesn't passively wait for a connection to magically appear. It rises. It seeks. It protects. It refuses to let busyness or routine steal the delight of being together.

That's why the Song repeatedly gives this wise warning: "I adjure you… that you not stir up or awaken love until it pleases" (Song of Solomon 2:7; also 3:5, 8:4). In marriage, this becomes a call to guard the sacred time you carve out together. The "little foxes" of distractions, unaddressed tension, or taking each other for granted can quietly spoil the blossoms of intimacy if left unchecked (Song of Solomon 2:15). Protect what God has planted.

You have 168 hours in a week. Your calendar doesn't lie. It reveals what you really value more than your words or good intentions ever could.

You're not "too busy." You're simply not prioritizing your marriage above the other good (but lesser) things that clamor for your focus—work demands, kids' activities, endless scrolling, chores, or even good ministry opportunities.

Whatever consistently gets your best time gets the best of you. If your marriage is only receiving the tired leftovers at the end of the day, don't be surprised when connection feels weak and distant.

Quantity and Quality: You Need Both

Some couples comfort themselves by saying, "It's not about how much time—it's about quality time." That sounds reasonable, but it's incomplete.

You need both quantity *and* quality.

Strong bonds rarely bloom in five-minute fragments between soccer drop-off and bedtime. It needs space. Margin. Consistency. Psychologists and relationship experts say that couples who protect 8–15 hours per week of focused time together consistently report stronger emotional intimacy, laughter, and satisfaction.

But here's the important warning: time alone isn't enough.

You've probably lived this scene—sitting in the same room, both glued to your phones, "watching" the same show while barely speaking a meaningful word. That's proximity, not the "come away" invitation of the Song.

So what turns ordinary time into a life-giving connection that repeats the delight in Solomon's song?

The Three Ingredients of Connected Time

1. **Intimacy** – Real, vulnerable conversation about what's truly going on in your hearts, dreams, fears, and joys—not just surface logistics.
2. **Variety** – New experiences that break the rut of routine and spark new energy, memories, and that sense of "the time of singing has come."
3. **Fun** – Because joy and playful delight are oxygen to a marriage. When fun fades, so do pursuit and passion.

Date Night: *-One of the Most Powerful Tools*

Here's what nobody tells you: Date Night isn't dead. You just forgot what it actually is.

- Remember when you were dating? Remember the electricity of waiting for Friday night? The way you'd check your phone every five minutes, hoping for a text or a call. The hours you'd spend getting ready, choosing the right outfit, rehearsing what you'd say. You were consumed. Obsessed. Nothing else mattered—not work stress, not bills, not what anyone else thought. Just the two of you and the intoxicating possibility of what you were building together. You weren't distracted. You weren't half-present. You didn't scroll Instagram while together. You were **all in.**

And somewhere between "I do" and now, you lost that intensity. Not because you stopped loving each other—but because you stopped protecting what made you fall in love in the first place.

Here's the brutal truth for most couples:

Jennsey and I were out recently at a nice restaurant—the kind of place you'd expect to see romance, connection, couples leaning in close. Instead, we watched couple after couple sit in silence, both scrolling their phones. One couple never looked up once during their entire meal. A family of four—mom, dad, two kids—all on devices, never speaking, never laughing, never even acknowledging each other's existence.

And the couples who *were* talking? They were arguing. Rehashing the same fight they've been having for months. Stress. Schedules. Money. The same exhausting loop.

Most Date Nights are really just eating dinner in public.

And if you're honest, you've done it too. You've sat across from your spouse and felt the awkward silence. You've pulled out your phone to fill the gap. You've talked about bills and kids' schedules because you didn't know what else to say anymore.

But here's what you need to understand: **You're not broken. You've just forgotten the rules.**

Because there was a time when you knew exactly how to do this. When you were dating, you didn't bring up stressful topics. You didn't check your phone every thirty seconds. You didn't talk about who spent what money or whose turn it was to do the dishes.

You **dreamed** together.

You talked about the future you were hoping to build. You laughed until your sides hurt. You flirted. You leaned in. You couldn't wait to see each other again.

That version of you still exists. You just buried it under ten years of logistics and exhaustion.

And here's the game-changing truth: **You can get it back. Starting this week.**

The Simple Model of A REAL DATE NIGHT

This isn't complicated. But it has to be non-negotiable.

1. **Put it on the calendar and protect it as if your life depended on it.** Because your marriage does.

   Every single week. No exceptions. Not "when things calm down." Not "if we can find a babysitter." Every.

Single. Week. If you don't make it a priority, life will devour it like a hot donut at a staff meeting.

1. **No phones. No kids. No distractions. No heavy problem-solving allowed.** This is sacred time.

- Not logistics planning time. Not stress-dumping time. Not bill-paying time.

If you start talking about the mortgage or the kids' report cards, Date Night is over. Pack it up. Go home. There are 167 other hours in the week to handle that stuff. This time is just for the two of you—flirting, laughing, remembering why you first fell in love, and finding new reasons to keep choosing each other.

1. **This is about pursuit. About presence. About being all in again.** Look at each other. Really look. Ask questions you haven't asked in years. Dream out loud. Be playful. Be curious. Be the version of yourself that made your spouse fall in love with you in the first place.

Here's what happens when you actually do this:

One couple we knew hit rock bottom. They were roommates managing a household, not lovers building a life. The spark was gone. The laughter had faded. They were one more silent dinner away from giving up.

Then they made one decision: **Friday nights became mandatory Date Night. No exceptions.**

At first? It felt awkward. Forced. They didn't know what to talk about. They felt like strangers trying to remember how to connect.

But both decided the fight was worth it, because it was a covenant not a contract.

And slowly—over time—something shifted.

They started laughing again. Real laughter, not polite chuckles. They started dreaming again about trips they wanted to take, goals they wanted to chase, and the life they still wanted to build together. The emotional distance that had formed over years of survival mode began to melt away.

Friday nights became the highlight of their week. Not because they went somewhere fancy. Not because they spent a lot of money. But because they finally obeyed the invitation to "arise... and come away."

They chose each other. On purpose. Every single week.

And their marriage came back to life.

The Hard Truth We Need to Hear

- **If you don't fight for time together, everything else in life will gladly steal it from you.** Your job will take it. Your kids will take it. Netflix will take it.

Exhaustion will take it. And one day you'll wake up and realize you're strangers living in the same house.

- **No one drifts into a great marriage. You build it. You protect it. You make it a priority—on purpose and consistently.** The couples with thriving marriages aren't lucky. They're not special. They just decided their marriage was worth protecting, and they built rhythms that made connection inevitable.

- **Time is not neutral. Every single week, it is either strengthening your marriage... or slowly weakening it.** There's no middle ground. You're either building closeness or allowing distance. You're either choosing each other or choosing everything else.

- **If you use Date Night to talk about bills, schedules, and stress, you might as well stay home. Date Night is over.** There is plenty of time to handle logistics. But only one chance each week to get this right. To remember why you chose each other. To rebuild what's been fading.

This is your wake-up call.

Your marriage might be slipping away—not because of one catastrophic moment, but because of a thousand small choices to prioritize everything else. And if you don't change course now, you could wake up five years from now, wondering where the person you married went.

But here's the hope: **It's not too late. You can choose differently. Starting this week.**

Put Date Night on the calendar. **Protect it. Show up. Be present. Be playful. Be all in**.

Because the marriage you want—the one you dreamed about when you were dating before marriage—is still possible.

But only if you fight for it.

The winter of distance doesn't have to last. The season of singing can come again. The flowers can bloom once more.

But only if you choose to rise. Only if you choose to protect the sacred time that keeps love alive.

This is worth fighting for.

So tonight, put down the phone. Look your spouse in the eyes. And say yes to the invitation.

Arise... and come away.

It's Your move.

TALK ABOUT IT

1. **If you pulled up your calendar right now and looked at the last month, would it show that your marriage is actually a top priority?**
    Not what you meant—what it shows. How much distraction-free time did you spend together (not just in the same room)? What got protected, and what got bumped? What is your calendar saying about your marriage right now?

2. **What's currently stealing the time you should be protecting for your marriage, and why are you letting it?**
    Be specific: work, kids' activities, screens, hobbies, friendships, or exhaustion. Which one is most responsible right now? What would it cost to say no— and what will it cost your marriage if you don't?

3. **When you think about "connected time" with your spouse, which of the three ingredients is missing most—intimacy, variety, or fun?**
    Which one do you need most right now—and why? Ask each other: "What would it look like to bring that back this week, and what do you need from me?"

CHAPTER 10

THE RHYTHM OF COMMUNICATION

If there is one area where marriages quietly fall apart, it's here.

You can survive a brutal work schedule. You can weather financial pressure or the turmoil of raising teenagers. You can even navigate seasons of deep stress and exhaustion.

But when communication breaks down, everything else eventually follows.

I'll never forget the story of Lewis and Elena. They had been married seventeen years and still sat opposite each other at dinner every night. From the outside, they looked fine—polite, functional, even friendly. But inside, they were starving.

One Thursday evening, Lewis sat across from Elena at their kitchen table. She was scrolling through her phone between bites of pasta, her face lit by the blue glow of the screen. He watched her for a moment—this woman he'd promised his life to—and felt something tighten in his chest.

He tried.

"How was your day?" he asked, keeping his voice light.

"Busy," she said without looking up. "Kids had practice. Dinner's in the fridge if you want more."

He nodded. Took another bite. Tried again.

"Anything... on your mind? Anything you're thinking about?"

Elena glanced up briefly, gave a small shrug. "Not really. Just tired."

And then she went back to her phone.

Lewis sat there, fork in hand, staring at the woman across from him. And in that moment, a thought hit him that made his stomach drop:

I'm sitting across from someone I love, and I have no idea what she's actually thinking.

He didn't know what was scaring her. He didn't know what she was hoping for. He didn't know if she was happy, lonely, frustrated, or just numb.

He was married to a stranger.

And the worst part? He couldn't remember when it had started. Had they always missed each other like this? Or had they just... stopped trying?

Lewis set his fork down and looked at his plate. The silence between them felt heavier than any argument they'd ever had.

Because at least in a fight, you're *trying* to reach each other.

This? This was two people existing in the same space, going through the motions, but completely alone.

They were talking. They just weren't *communicating*.

Early in their marriage, everything had flowed out—dreams, fears, silly private jokes, late-night hopes for the future. Now conversations rarely went deeper than logistics, complaints, or quick updates. Vulnerability had quietly walked out the door. Intimacy followed soon after.

They weren't angry. They weren't in crisis. They had simply slipped into exchanging information instead of understanding and being understood.

This is where most couples miss it.

The Slow Shift

At first, communication feels effortless. You talk about everything. You finish each other's sentences. You ask curious questions because you genuinely want to know the heart behind the words.

But over time, life gets loud. Fatigue sets in. The deep talks give way to surface-level interactions. You move from sharing souls to managing schedules. You're still interacting—but you're no longer connecting.

And when vulnerability leaves, intimacy isn't far behind.

Why This Happens

Deep communication takes effort. It requires presence, patience, emotional energy, and deliberate focus. Most evenings, you're tired, distracted, or preoccupied. So instead of leaning in, you default to what's easy: short answers, quick updates, avoiding anything that might lead to conflict.

Until one day you wake up and realize, "We don't really talk like we used to."

That's not random. That's a pattern. And patterns always produce outcomes.

The 10-Minute Rule

The National Institute of Health and Phycology Today shows that even just ten minutes of real, focused conversation a day can dramatically increase intimacy and connection. Not multitasking. Not side-by-side scrolling. Focused. Undistracted. Heart-to-heart.

Yet most couples don't do it. Not because they don't care, but because they don't protect the time or the posture.

Here's the shift that changes everything: stop trying to *be heard* and start trying to *understand.*

Conversations stop being battles to win and become bridges between us.

What Breaks Communication

Most communication problems boil down to this: we're more focused on defending ourselves than discovering our spouse.

We react instead of respond. We correct instead of exploring. We assume instead of asking.

Dangerous assumptions creep in: "What I say is more important than how I say it." "If we're really close, they should just know what I mean."

Those beliefs destroy connection. Tone matters. Clarity matters. Intent matters. Mind-reading always leads to frustration.

The Shift: From Reacting to Loving

If you want better communication in your marriage, filter everything through what Paul calls the Love Lens—**1 Corinthians 13:4-8**.

Love is patient, love is kind. It does not envy, it does not boast, it is not proud. It does not dishonor others, It is not self-seeking, It is not easily angered, it keeps no record of wrongs. Love does not delight in evil but rejoices with the truth. It always protects, always trusts, always hopes, always perseveres. Love never fails.

This is where maturity shows up. When you communicate with your spouse, filter everything through this lens to determine if you are loving your spouse or not. It's not hard to understand, it's just hard to actually do.

Proverbs 18:21 - The tongue has the power of life and death…

It's no secret that the tongue has incredible power. Our words can encourage and build up, as well as deeply wound those we love the most. The unfortunate reality is that when our words wound, we can never unsay the hurt, even in the midst of regret.

Four Practical Tips That Change Everything

1. **Focused Attention:** Put the phone down. Make eye contact. Give your spouse your full attention. They can tell when they're competing with a screen, and if they keep losing, they may stop trying to get your attention.

2. **Clear Expectations:** Many conflicts aren't about big issues—they're about misunderstood expectations. Instead of assuming your spouse sees things the same way, ask, "What does that look like to you?" Being clear can prevent many arguments.

3. **Second Question:** This simple habit is powerful. Instead of jumping in with your response, slow down and ask a follow-up question: "What did that feel like for you?" "Why did that matter so much?" "Can you help me understand more?" These questions show you care enough to go deeper, and they build trust quickly.

4. **Positive, Life-Giving Language:** Scripture is clear about this. Ephesians 4:29 says, "Let no corrupting talk come out of your mouths, but only such as is good for building up, as fits the occasion, that it may give grace to those who hear."

Compare: "You never help me around the house" vs. "I feel overwhelmed—can you help me with this?"

Same issue. Completely different outcome. A gentle tongue brings healing (Proverbs 15:4). Rash words cut like a sword, but wise words restore (Proverbs 12:18). James 1:19 urges us to be "quick to hear, slow to speak, slow to anger."

You don't get better responses by increasing pressure. You get them by improving your approach.

The Hard Truth

If your communication doesn't change, your marriage won't either.

You can fix schedules and modify priorities, but if you keep reacting, defending, and assuming instead of listening, understanding, and responding with grace, you'll keep running into the same walls in different situations.

Communication is never neutral. Every single day, it is either strengthening your relationship... or slowly weakening it.

BUBBLE TIME

We call it Bubble Time because that's exactly what it is—a protected bubble of time where nothing else exists. So let me paint a picture for you.

You know how, when a couple seems to be upset with each other, the frustration seems to have more power in the marriage than anything else. Both just walk around with an attitude, waiting for the moment they can emphasize their frustration.

Husbands even work late to avoid coming home too early and have to endure the same old argument about the same old things. They would rather come home late and only have to endure it for 2 hours instead of 4. If they do come home sooner, they feel like they are walking on eggshells until it's time to go to bed.

Wives walk around wondering if the man they are married to will ever start leading like they need him to. They are also scared that he will never stop and have a real conversation with them, which would help them understand how he is processing life. All they think is that he is processing life without them.

So, this is where Bubble Time comes in. Bubble Time is a protected time just like Date Night. You set it up like this:

1. Choose a time (set a consistent day and time every week).

   - Ie. EVERY THURSDAY – 8:00PM – LIVING ROOM
   - Kids need to be in bed, phones turned off, no visitors.

2. Get a Yellow Legal pad with a magnet. Put it in the refrigerator.

   - This pad is where you write down all the issues of the week. When you find yourselves starting to argue about money or anything, you get to call an audible and say, "Put it on the pad."
   - Now here's the key. Once it goes on the pad, no one can bring it up until Bubble Time.
   - Here's the other key. EVERYONE HAS TO SHOW UP for Bubble Time. No excuses. It has to happen, or this doesn't work.

3. BUBBLE TIME (day/night) - NO Phones, NO Kids, NO Excuses

4. Pray a simple prayer over your time.

   - ***God, please help us to love each other well, give us guidance and wisdom as we honor you with our words and intentions. Amen.***

5. Come with this understanding: your spouse isn't the enemy. The issues on the pad are. Tackle what you can

in the time you've set, prioritizing the most important
first.

6. Once the pad goes back on the refrigerator, it's off
    limits until next Bubble Time.

Here's where the magic happens. You'll write something in
anger on Tuesday—maybe about your spouse always being on
their phone during dinner. But by Thursday, you've realized it
wasn't even the real issue, or you've already let it go. That's the
beauty of Bubble Time.

When you sit down to talk, half the pad is already resolved.
You'll flip through and realize some things embarrassed you
the moment you wrote them down. Other items? They've
already worked themselves out because you had time to cool
off and think clearly.

It's always fun to see how conversations start when so many
items are already marked off.

Bubble Time is good for everything. Money Talks, Calendars,
Time, Kids, etc.

The Good News

Bubble Time is one of the fastest ways to improve
communication—if you're willing to be intentional.

Start tonight. Put the phones away. Look your spouse in the
eyes.

Give efforts to ask good second questions and speak words that build up and give grace.

You don't have to be perfect. You just have to be willing.

Final Question

Be honest with yourself right now: Are your conversations building connection... or slowly breaking it down?

The words you choose today are forming the marriage you'll live in tomorrow.

Your marriage is listening.

TALK ABOUT IT

1. **If you're brutally honest, what do most of your conversations look like—deep and vulnerable, or surface-level and transactional?**
   Over the last week: how often did you share what's really in your heart?

2. **What keeps you from being truly vulnerable with your spouse—fear of judgment, past hurts, exhaustion, or something else?**
   Identify what's holding you back, then ask: "What do you need from me to feel safe enough to be fully honest?"

3. **When your spouse shares something important, do you listen to understand—or to defend, fix, and respond?**

   Be honest: when they share something hard, is your first instinct to explain, solve it so the conversation ends, or justify yourself—rather than hear their heart?

THE RHYTHM OF FRIENDSHIP

Ethan and Rebekah sat across from each other at a nice restaurant—the kind with cloth napkins and candlelight. Date night. They'd protected the time, hired the sitter, dressed up. They were doing everything "right."

But twenty minutes in, the silence between them felt heavier than the conversation.

They'd covered the basics: how the kids were doing, what needed to be fixed around the house, whether they should refinance. Practical. Necessary. Boring.

Ethan looked at his wife—the woman he'd once stayed up until 3 a.m. talking to, the one who used to make him laugh until his stomach hurt—and realized something that made his chest tighten.

We've become boring. Not to the world. To each other.

They weren't fighting. They weren't in crisis. They were just... flat. The spark that used to make everything feel alive had dimmed to something that felt more like obligation than joy.

Rebekah felt it too. She looked down at her plate and said quietly, "Do you ever feel like we've forgotten how to have fun?"

Ethan didn't answer right away. Because the truth was yes. And admitting it out loud felt like confessing failure.

They'd built a life together—a good one. But somewhere along the way, they'd stopped enjoying it. Stopped enjoying *each other*.

They'd become roommates managing a household instead of friends building a life.

And that realization—quiet, painful, undeniable—became their breaking point.

When Marriage Loses Friendship

Here's what most couples don't realize until it's too late: **You can have commitment without connection. You can have partnership without pleasure. You can have a marriage that functions... but doesn't feel alive.**

And when friendship fades, everything else starts to break down.

Conflict feels more threatening because you're not sure your spouse actually *likes* you anymore.

Vulnerability feels riskier because you've lost the safety that comes from knowing someone genuinely enjoys being with you.

Hard seasons feel heavier because you're carrying the weight together, but you're not laughing together anymore.

Friendship isn't the icing on the cake of marriage. It's the foundation everything else is built on.

Without it, marriage becomes transactional. Routine. Disconnected.

You do life side by side, but you're not actually *with* each other.

The Question That Changes Everything

We know another couple—Marcel and Elena—who hit this same wall after sixteen years of marriage.

They weren't fighting. They were polite, cooperative, functional. But one night, after the kids were in bed, Marcel looked at Elena and asked a question that cracked everything open:

"Do you even like spending time with me anymore?"

Elena's first instinct was to say, *Of course I do.* But she stopped herself. Because if she was honest, she wasn't sure.

She loved him. She was committed to him. But *like* him? Enjoy being with him?

When was the last time they'd laughed together—really laughed, not just polite chuckles at something one of the kids said?

When was the last time they'd done something just because it sounded fun, not because it was on the to-do list?

When was the last time she'd looked forward to being alone with him instead of feeling relieved when he went to bed early?

The silence that followed Marcel's question was answer enough.

And that's when they realized: **They'd stopped being friends.**

What Friendship Actually Requires

Friendship in marriage doesn't happen by accident. It doesn't maintain itself. It requires three things most couples stop protecting:

1. Time (Not Just Proximity)

You can live in the same house, sleep in the same bed, and still be strangers. Proximity isn't connection.

Friendship requires time where you're actually *present* to each other—not distracted, not multitasking, not half-listening while scrolling your phone.

Time where the goal isn't to solve a problem or check something off the list. Time where you're together just because you want to be.

2. Intentionality (Choosing to Engage)

Friendship doesn't survive on autopilot. You have to choose it.

You have to choose to ask the question that goes deeper than "How was your day?"

You have to choose to laugh at the joke even when you're tired.

You have to choose to say yes to the spontaneous idea even when the couch sounds easier.

Friendship is built in the small moments when you choose engagement over convenience.

3. Lightness (Letting Go of Heaviness)

Marriage carries weight—bills, decisions, conflict, responsibility. And if every conversation is heavy, friendship suffocates under the pressure.

You need space to be light together. To play. To be silly. To let go of the seriousness and just enjoy each other.

Laughter isn't a luxury in marriage. It's oxygen.

And when you stop laughing together, you start dying together—slowly, quietly, without even realizing it.

The Three-Part Rhythm of Friendship

So how do you rebuild friendship when it's been fading for years?

The same way you build anything in marriage: **through rhythm.**

Not grand gestures. Not expensive vacations. Not waiting until you "feel like it."

Small, intentional, repeated moments that create space for joy to return.

Here's the rhythm that works:

One Moment a Day (30-Second Connection)

This is the smallest investment with the biggest return. Thirty seconds of intentional lightness.

A joke texted in the middle of the day. A playful comment when you're making dinner. A quick dance in the kitchen to a song on the radio. A compliment that has nothing to do with what your spouse *does* and everything to do with who they *are*.

It sounds insignificant. But these micro-moments are what keep friendship alive when everything else is pulling you apart.

Ethan started texting Rebekah memes that made him think of her. Stupid, random, completely unnecessary. But every time her phone buzzed and she saw his name, she smiled.

That thirty-second moment reminded her: *He's thinking about me. He wants to make me laugh.*

And slowly, the distance between them started to shrink.

One Night a Week (Protected Fun)

This is Date Night, but with a specific rule: **No heavy topics allowed.**

No talking about the budget. No processing conflict. No solving problems.

This night is for *enjoying* each other, not managing each other.

Marcel and Elena started playing cards every Thursday night after the kids went to bed. Nothing fancy. Just Rummy or Uno at the kitchen table.

At first, it felt forced. Awkward. Like they were trying too hard.

But then Elena made a joke about Marcel's terrible poker face, and he laughed—really laughed—and suddenly the tension broke.

They started trash-talking each other. Keeping ridiculous score. Making up absurd rules just to mess with each other.

And for the first time in years, they weren't *working* on their marriage. They were just... having fun.

That's when Elena realized: *I actually like this man.*

Not just love him. *Like* him.

And that changed everything.

One Memory a Month (Something New)

Friendship grows stale when life becomes predictable. You need new experiences to create new stories.

Once a month, do something you've never done together.

It doesn't have to be expensive or elaborate. It just has to be *new*.

Try a recipe you've never made and laugh when it turns out terrible. Drive to a part of town you've never explored and walk around like tourists. Take a dance class and stumble through the steps together. Go to a bookstore and pick out books for each other. Hike a trail you've been talking about for years but never actually did.

The goal isn't perfection. It's *shared experience*.

Because when you create new memories together, you're reminded that your story isn't finished. You're still writing it.

Ethan and Rebekah started trying new restaurants once a month—nothing fancy, just places they'd never been. One night they ended up at a tiny Thai place that was way spicier than they expected, and they spent the whole meal laughing, crying, and chugging water.

It was ridiculous. Uncomfortable. Completely unplanned.

And it became one of their favorite memories.

Not because the food was good. Because they were *present* to each other in a way they hadn't been in years.

How Friendship Makes Everything Else Work

Here's what Marcel and Elena discovered as they rebuilt friendship through these rhythms:

Conflict felt less threatening because they knew their spouse actually liked them. Disagreements didn't feel like rejection anymore—they felt like two friends working through a problem.

Vulnerability felt less risky because they'd rebuilt the safety that comes from knowing someone enjoys being with you. Sharing hard things didn't feel like burdening their spouse—it felt like trusting a friend.

Hard seasons felt less heavy because they were carrying the weight together *and* laughing together. The pressure didn't disappear, but it didn't crush them either.

Friendship didn't solve all their problems. But it made everything else easier to navigate.

Because when you genuinely like the person you're married to, you fight harder to protect what you have.

Our Story: Protecting Fun Fiercely

We've learned this the hard way in our own marriage.

There have been seasons where we were so focused on building, leading, parenting, and managing that we forgot to *enjoy* each other.

We were committed. We were aligned. We were working together.

But we weren't having fun.

And when fun fades, so does the aliveness that makes marriage feel like a gift instead of a grind.

So we made a decision: **We would protect fun as fiercely as we protect anything else.**

We keep a running list on our phones of things we want to try—restaurants, hikes, games, random ideas that sound interesting.

We say yes to spontaneous moments even when we're tired.

We choose laughter over efficiency, even when there's still work to be done.

Because we've learned that the work will always be there. But the moments to connect? Those disappear if you don't fight for them.

And here's what we've noticed: **The weeks we laugh together are the weeks everything else feels lighter.**

Not because the pressure decreased. Because we're carrying it as friends, not just partners.

The Legacy of Friendship

A few months ago, our daughter said something that stopped us in our tracks.

We were talking about marriage, and she said, "I want a marriage like yours. You guys actually seem like you *like* each other."

Not just love. *Like.*

She'd been watching. And what she saw wasn't perfection. It was friendship.

She saw us laughing in the kitchen. Dancing badly to old songs. Teasing each other over dinner. Choosing joy even when life was hard.

And that became her picture of what marriage should look like.

Not just commitment. Not just responsibility. Not just surviving together.

But actually *enjoying* the person you chose.

That's the legacy friendship creates.

Your kids—your friends, your community—are watching. And they're learning what marriage is supposed to feel like by watching yours.

Are they learning that marriage is heavy, serious, and exhausting?

Or are they learning that marriage can be joyful, playful, and alive?

You Can Get It Back. But Not By Waiting.

If you're reading this and thinking, *We've lost that. We don't laugh anymore. We don't enjoy each other like we used to,* here's what you need to know:

You can get it back. But not by waiting for it to return on its own. Not by hoping the spark magically reignites. Not by assuming it'll get better when life calms down.

You get it back the same way you lost it: **through small, repeated choices.**

You lost it by choosing work over play, efficiency over presence, seriousness over silliness.

You get it back by choosing differently. One joke. One game night. One new experience. Repeated. Protected. Prioritized.

Friendship doesn't require a personality transplant or a complete life overhaul.

It just requires you to start choosing joy again.

Friendship Isn't a Luxury. It's Oxygen.

Here's the truth most couples miss: **Friendship isn't the bonus feature of a good marriage. It's the foundation everything else is built on.**

Without it, intimacy feels forced.

Without it, conflict feels dangerous.

Without it, hard seasons feel unbearable.

But *with* it? Everything changes.

Friendship Makes Hard Conversations Possible

Here's something most couples don't realize until it's too late: **When you genuinely like your spouse, conflict feels less like a threat and more like a problem you can solve together.**

Think about it. When you have a disagreement with a close friend—someone you genuinely enjoy being around—you don't assume the friendship is over. You don't spiral into "they don't love me anymore" or "this proves we're incompatible." You just think, *We see this differently. Let's figure it out.*

You can disagree and still like each other.

But when friendship is gone? Every disagreement feels like rejection. Every hard conversation feels like an attack. Because there's no reservoir of goodwill to draw from. No recent memory of laughter or lightness to remind you, *We're okay. We're on the same team.*

Friendship creates a kind of emotional bank account. And when that account is full—when you've been laughing together, enjoying each other, choosing fun over efficiency—you can have hard conversations without the whole relationship feeling fragile.

We've watched this play out in countless couples.

Take two marriages facing the exact same conflict: how to handle a difficult decision about aging parents.

Without friendship, the conversation sounds like this: tense voices, defensive postures, every word carefully chosen because one wrong phrase could ignite an argument. The issue isn't really about the parents—it's about all the unspoken resentment, the distance, the feeling that "you never listen to me anyway." The conversation ends with someone shutting down or walking away. Nothing gets resolved. The gap widens.

With friendship, the same conversation sounds completely different: "This is hard. I don't know the right answer. What do you think?" There's still tension—it's a difficult topic—but there's also trust. Safety. The ability to say, "I'm scared about this," without fear of being dismissed. And when voices get a little sharp, one of them can pause and say, "Hey, we're on the same team, remember?" And the other one softens. Because they actually believe it.

That's the difference friendship makes.

It's not that couples with strong friendship never fight. They do. But their fights don't threaten the foundation. Because underneath the disagreement is a bedrock of *I actually like you. I enjoy being with you. This conflict doesn't change that.*

And that changes everything.

This is why we moved this chapter earlier in the book. Because you can't build intimacy, navigate conflict, or practice vulnerability without this foundation. Friendship isn't the reward you get after you fix everything else. It's the soil everything else grows in.

Friendship isn't just about fun. It's the safety net that makes everything else possible.

When you like each other, you can be honest with each other. When you enjoy each other, you can be vulnerable without fear. When you're friends, hard seasons don't destroy you— they deepen you.

So if you've been trying to fix communication, rebuild intimacy, or resolve conflict without first rebuilding friendship, you're building on sand.

Start here. Rebuild the friendship. Protect the joy. Everything else will follow.

With friendship, you have a partner you actually want to be around. With friendship, you have safety to be vulnerable. With friendship, you have joy that sustains you when everything else is hard.

So if you've lost it, fight to get it back. If you still have it, protect it fiercely. Because the marriage you're building isn't just about surviving together. It's about *enjoying* the person you chose to build with. And that starts with friendship.

TALK ABOUT IT

1. **Be honest: Do you still *like* your spouse, or have you just been managing life together?**

   Think about the last month. When was the last time you genuinely enjoyed being with them—not because you were accomplishing something, but just because you wanted to be together?

2. **When did you stop having fun together, and what changed?**

   Try to pinpoint the season when laughter started fading. Was it after kids? A job change? A hard season? Identifying when helps you understand what needs to shift.

3. **What's one small, specific thing you could do this week to rebuild friendship—a joke, a game, a walk, a new experience?**

   Don't wait for the perfect moment. Pick one rhythm from this chapter (one moment daily, one night weekly, one memory monthly) and start this week. Friendship rebuilds through action, not intention.

CHAPTER 12

THE RHYTHM OF MONEY

Money doesn't just reveal problems in marriage; it also creates them. It exposes them.

You can hide a lot of issues for a while—courteous smiles, busy schedules, surface-level conversations. But bring up money, and everything surfaces: different values, hidden fears, old wounds, unspoken expectations, alongside the quiet question of who really owns what.

I'll never forget sitting with Jared and Megan. They'd been married eleven years—successful by every external measure. Nice home, two cars, kids in good schools. But behind closed doors, finances had become a constant battle. They were exhausted, disconnected, and stuck in a pattern they couldn't break.

Jared grew up in a home where money was always tight. His parents scraped by, and the fear of never having enough shaped him into the ultimate saver. Every extra dollar went into savings, investments, or "just in case." "We have to be responsible," he'd say with nervousness in his voice tone.

Megan grew up watching her parents enjoy life—family vacations, nice dinners, spontaneous adventures. To her, money was meant to create memories and bring joy. "We only live once," she'd counter. "Why save everything for the future that might never come?"

Their fights followed a painful script that repeated month after month.

She'd suggest something—a family vacation, furniture for the kids' rooms, even just a nicer dinner out. He'd do what he always did: pull up the budget spreadsheet, cite the numbers, explain why they couldn't afford it.

"We have to think about retirement," he'd say, his tone matter-of-fact.

"We are thinking about it," she'd counter. "But we're also living right now. Our kids will only be little once."

"Exactly. Which is why we need to be responsible. We can't just spend money every time we feel like it."

The word "just" landed like a slap. Like her wanting to create memories, to let their kids experience joy, was frivolous. Irresponsible. Wrong.

"I'm not talking about being reckless, Jared," she'd say, her voice getting quieter, which was somehow worse than yelling. "I'm talking about living. About enjoying the life we've worked so hard for. But with you, it's never enough. We're never safe enough. Never have enough. There's always some reason to say no."

And he'd withdraw. Because to him, she wasn't hearing him. She was dismissing the very real fear that had lived in his chest since childhood—the terror of not having enough, of everything crumbling, of ending up like his parents.

So he'd say nothing. Just close the spreadsheet and walk away. And Megan would be left sitting there, feeling unheard and controlled. Jared would be in the other room, feeling misunderstood and disrespected.

This cycle repeated month after month. Vacation brochures got quietly deleted. Ideas got swallowed before she even voiced them. He stopped trying to explain himself. She stopped trying to ask.

They weren't fighting anymore—they were just... distant. Moving around each other in the same house, managing logistics, but the partnership was eroding.

One night, Megan found a credit card bill. There was a charge from a golf outing Jared had taken with coworkers—$200, without discussion. She stared at it, something cracking inside her.

She'd asked him for a $150 new mattress for their daughter's room months ago. He'd said no, said they needed to save. But apparently golf was fine. Apparently his fun was the exception.

That night, she didn't stay calm. Years of unheard requests, dismissed dreams, and swallowed desires came pouring out.

"You won't let us live," she said, her voice shaking. "You control every dollar. And for what? So we can be miserable now and maybe comfortable in forty years? I don't want that. I don't want our kids to remember a parent who said no to everything. I want them to remember a mom and dad who chose them. Who chose us."

Jared's face hardened. "That's not fair. I'm trying to protect us."

"You're not protecting us," she said quietly. "You're protecting yourself. And it's killing us."

That silence afterward was the longest yet. Because she was right, and he knew it. But he didn't know how to fix it. The fear was too deep. The patterns were too old.

The next morning, Jared woke up realizing: his wife was giving up. Not on him, necessarily, but on the idea that they could ever be on the same page about money. And if money—the practical day-to-day decisions that shape life—kept dividing them, what did that mean for everything else?

Finally, that evening, instead of defending his position or recounting her recklessness, Jared sat down exhausted and raw. For the first time, they talked about their childhood stories with money—not to win the argument, but to sincerely understand each other's hearts. Jared shared the deep fear of ending up like his parents, always scraping by. Megan shared her fear of looking back on life with regret, having never truly lived or made memories.

That honest conversation didn't magically fix their budget. But it changed the atmosphere. They stopped seeing each other as opponents and began seeing money as something they were called to steward *together* under God's ownership. The shift from "mine vs. yours" to "ours under God" opened the door to real unity.

The Beat That Changes Everything

Building unity around money doesn't happen by accident or good intentions. It requires a clear, repeatable rhythm grounded in stewardship.

Main Goal – GET ON THE SAME PAGE

1. **Common Vision** — Before you touch a spreadsheet or budget, get on the same page about your future as stewards. Pray together and ask the big questions:
   - Where do we believe God is leading our family in the next five, ten, or twenty years?
- What matters most—experiences that build memories, security for the future, generosity that advances God's kingdom, or simplicity that frees us to serve?
   - How can our finances reflect our love for God and others?

1. **Written Plan (Budget)** — If it's not written down, you won't stick to it. A budget is not a prison sentence—it's insight and freedom. It tells your money where to go instead of wondering where it went. Start simple and honest. It doesn't have to be perfect on day one. Consistency matters more than precision.

2. **Monthly Money Meeting** — This is essential for good stewardship. Schedule a calm, distraction-free time each month—no kids, no phones, no raised voices. Review spending from the previous month, adjust the plan as needed, address concerns with grace, and celebrate small wins together. Keep it focused and short. The goal is alignment and faithfulness, not winning.

These three rhythms—vision, plan, and regular accountability—turn money conversations from battles into teamwork. But they only work when you approach them with grace.

The Real Issue

You will not agree on everything. That's normal. But refusing to move toward each other is the problem. Healthy stewardship requires give and take—sometimes you adjust, sometimes your spouse does—but you always move closer together. Prioritize generosity (Proverbs 3:9). Practice contentment (Hebrews 13:5). And remember the parable of the talents: faithfulness with what you have now opens the door to greater trust from the Master (Matthew 25:14-30).

If money is a constant source of tension, stop and ask: Is this really a money problem, or a stewardship and unity problem?

Here's what's actually at stake: your trust in each other, the spiritual foundation you're building for your children, and the legacy you're leaving. Every time you fight over money without alignment, you're teaching your kids that resources divide instead of unite. You're modeling fear instead of faith.

When you're aligned as stewards—God at the center, both managing His resources with open hands—decisions become easier, stress drops, and trust grows. Not because circumstances are perfect, but because you're on the same team with the same mission: faithfulness to the One who owns it all. The scorekeeping stops. Money becomes a tool for building together instead of a weapon in a quiet war.

You don't have to stay stuck. The shift is available right now—not someday when finances are easier. Today.

The Good News

Jared and Megan are living proof. After months of honest conversations, shared prayer, and consistent stewardship meetings, their money rhythm began working *for* them instead of against them. They still have different tendencies—one saver, one enjoyer—but now they steward those differences together. Vacations happen with wisdom. Savings grow with peace. Generosity flows with joy. And their marriage is stronger because of it.

Are you managing money together as faithful stewards of what belongs to God... or just coexisting around it, keeping separate scorecards?

Those are two very different realities. The longer you avoid true alignment, the more pressure builds. But when you make this shift—when you stop clutching resources as owners and start releasing them as stewards—you don't just reduce financial stress. You build lasting trust, deep unity, and shared direction that strengthens every other rhythm in your marriage.

Your money is not just about numbers. It's about values, dreams, faithfulness, and legacy.

Choose to build the rhythm of stewardship now.

Your marriage—and your eternity—is worth the honest, grace-filled work.

TALK ABOUT IT

1. **Describe your money personalities—and what shaped them.**

   Name your tendencies (saver/spender, planner/spontaneous, tight-fisted/open-handed) and the family patterns behind them (scarcity/abundance, conflict/peace, control/freedom). Share the "why" so you respond with understanding, not conflict.

2. **Are you living as owners or stewards?**

   Where are you still operating from "mine vs. yours" (spending without agreement, resentment, control)? Name one concrete step you'll take this month to manage God's resources together.

3. **What does your spending reveal about your priorities and love for God?**

   Review your statements: what do they show (generosity or self-focus, intention or drift, trust or fear, unity or competition)? Identify one change to better align your spending with your faith.

CHAPTER 13

THE RHYTHM OF ADVENTURE

Most marriages, that crumble, don't fall apart because of explosive conflict. They fade because of complacency.

Not because of fighting. Not because of breaking. Just... slowly losing life.

One day, you look across the table at the person and realize the relationship feels flat. Safe, maybe. Predictable, definitely. But alive? Not so much.

Ryan and Lauren had been married fourteen years.

Three kids. A house they'd just paid off. Careers that were stable. A life that looked, from the outside, like everything was working.

But something had died between them.

Not their love—they still loved each other. Not their commitment—they weren't going anywhere. But the spark? The aliveness? That had quietly slipped away.

Weekends looked identical: chores, kids' activities, takeout on the couch, scrolling phones until bedtime. Date nights had become routine dinners-and-a-movie, where they mostly talked about schedules and the kids. The spontaneous road trips, silly inside jokes, and late-night dreams they once shared had quietly disappeared.

They still loved each other. They were committed. But somewhere along the way, they had traded adventure for comfort—and comfort was slowly suffocating their connection.

What Ryan and Lauren were experiencing wasn't unique. It's what happens when couples forget that marriage—the way God designed it—was never meant to be static. Scripture shows us that marriage reflects the faithful, creative love between God and His people (Ephesians 5:25–32). It's a dynamic partnership, not a destination you arrive at and coast through.

Even when life looks successful on paper, genuine flourishing requires intentional spiritual practices, shared experiences that honor God, and ongoing pursuit of each other's hearts and dreams.

Ryan later confessed, "We stopped pursuing each other the day we said 'I do.' We thought marriage meant we had arrived. Instead, we just stopped growing."

When We Stop Adventuring, We Stop Growing

Remember the beginning?

You stayed up until 3 a.m. talking about everything and nothing. You drove two hours just to see a band you'd never heard of. You laughed until your stomach hurt over inside jokes no one else understood. You made plans—wild, beautiful, impossible plans—and believed you could do anything together.

You were *alive*.

Now? You can barely remember the last time you had a conversation that wasn't about the calendar or the kids. The last time you laughed—really laughed—together. The last time you felt that spark of "we're in this adventure together."

Here's what happened: You stopped adventuring together. And when adventure stopped, growth stopped. And when growth stopped, connection began to fade.

Not all at once. Slowly. Quietly. Like a fire you forgot to tend.

You told yourself it was maturity. Responsibility. Being realistic. But deep down, you know the truth: life has become predictable. Safe. Flat.

And flat is killing you both.

You weren't designed for a boring marriage. God didn't create you to coast through life on autopilot, checking boxes and counting down to retirement. He designed marriage to be dynamic—a partnership where two people pursue each other, dream together, and keep choosing aliveness over comfort.

The good news? That aliveness isn't gone. It's just waiting for you to choose it again.

What Adventure Really Is

Here's the relief: Adventure isn't about quitting your job or selling everything you own. It's not about backpacking through Europe or learning to skydive.

Adventure is a *mindset.*

It's the choice to say "yes" when comfort whispers "stay safe." It's choosing the new restaurant over the usual Friday night takeout. Growth over autopilot. Intentionality over passivity. Curiosity over predictability.

It's deciding that your marriage deserves more than what's left over after everything else gets your best energy.

Think about it: From the very beginning, God placed Adam and Eve in a garden bursting with variety—endless beauty to discover, endless possibilities to explore. He didn't put them in a beige waiting room. He gave them a world of wonder and told them to be fruitful, to create, to explore, to steward life *together* (Genesis 1:28).

That calling didn't expire at the altar.

God designed your marriage to be alive—dynamic, creative, growing. Not a museum where you preserve what once was, but a garden where you cultivate what's still becoming.

Adventure isn't an escape from your real life. It's the refusal to let your real life become a slow fade into nothing.

Comfort feels safe, but it slowly kills momentum. You stop trying as hard. You stop pursuing. You stop paying attention. Not intentionally—just gradually. And when pursuit stops, connection weakens.

Because what you don't actively build, you slowly lose.

You Have to Keep the Chase Alive

This is where most couples get it wrong. They think, "We're married now. We've won. We can relax."

No. You don't stop pursuing your spouse the day you say "I do." You pursue them *because* you chose them—and that pursuit should never end. Familiarity should lead to deeper connection, not replace effort.

The Song of Solomon captures this beautifully. The lover doesn't settle once he "has" his bride. He continues to chase, to invite, to delight: "Arise, my love... and come away" (Song of Solomon 2:10). Even after marriage, the pursuit remains alive and passionate.

The Role of Shared Experiences

New experiences reignite connection because they break the rut of routine, create fresh memories you'll talk about for years, spark emotion and laughter, and build a sense of "us against the world."

You remember moments, not routines. And most couples today are running on routines with very few meaningful shared moments. That's why things feel dull.

Dreams That Make Your Spouse Come Alive

Do you know your spouse's dreams—the ones that make their eyes light up? Most couples used to know them... and then stopped asking.

Life got busy. Responsibilities piled up. Dreams got shelved.

But marriage was never meant to suppress dreams. It was meant to support them. When you stop asking about what makes your spouse come alive, they start to believe you don't care. That who they're becoming doesn't matter to you.

That's heartbreaking. And it's fixable.

Healthy marriages don't just tolerate dreams—they water them. You ask about them. You pay attention when your spouse's eyes light up. You create space for what makes them come alive.

Try this: Once a month, look your spouse in the eye and ask, "What's one dream you have right now that you haven't told me about?"

Then do the hardest thing: *listen*. Really listen. Not with your phone in your hand. Not while planning your response. Listen like their answer matters—because it does.

Then find even one small way to water that dream. Maybe it's giving them an afternoon to pursue it. Maybe it's asking a follow-up question next week. Maybe it's just saying, "I love seeing you come alive when you talk about this."

Ryan and Lauren sat in their living room on a Tuesday night, fourteen years into a marriage that looked perfect on paper but felt hollow inside. They had the house. The kids. The stability. Everything they thought they wanted.

But they couldn't remember the last time they'd laughed together. Really laughed. The last time they'd stayed up late talking about something that mattered.

That night, Ryan asked Lauren the question: "What's one dream you have that I haven't asked about?"

She cried. Not because the question was hard—but because she couldn't remember the last time he'd asked.

She told him about the pottery class she'd been thinking about for two years. How she drove past the studio every week and imagined what it would feel like to create something with her hands again. How she'd convinced herself it was silly. Selfish. A waste of time.

Ryan signed her up the next day.

When your spouse feels seen and supported in what makes them come alive, your marriage comes alive too. You stop being roommates managing a life together and become partners championing each other toward who you're meant to be.

Permission to Change

Here's something most couples never talk about: You are not married to the same person you said "I do" to.

The woman who walked down the aisle ten years ago? She's not the same woman sitting across from you tonight. The man who promised forever? He's grown, shifted, discovered new parts of himself you never saw coming.

And that's not a problem. That's *life*.

But somewhere along the way, you started expecting your spouse to stay frozen. To want the same things. To fit neatly into the role you assigned them on your wedding day.

And when they don't? When they mention a new interest, a different passion, a dream that doesn't fit your plan? You feel threatened. You resist.

You're not trying to be cruel. You're just scared. Because change feels like loss.

But here's the truth: when you try to control who your spouse is becoming, you don't preserve your marriage. You suffocate it.

Real love—the kind that lasts—gives permission. It says, "I see you changing, and I'm not afraid. I want to know this version of you too." It asks questions instead of shutting down. It celebrates growth instead of resisting it.

When you support your spouse's growth—when you make space for who they're becoming instead of clinging to who they were—you don't lose them. You get to fall in love with them all over again.

So ask yourself: Are you giving your spouse permission to grow? Or are you quietly demanding they stay the same so you don't have to stretch?

Because one breathes life and the other destroys it.

The Hard Truth

If your marriage has no adventure, it will eventually feel lifeless. Not broken. Not over. Just flat.

And flat marriages are vulnerable—because when some type of excitement comes from the outside, it becomes tempting.

That's real. That's why this matters.

Ryan and Lauren sat in their living room on a Tuesday night, fourteen years into a marriage that looked perfect on paper but felt hollow inside. They had the house. The kids. The stability. Everything they thought they wanted.

But they couldn't remember the last time they'd laughed together. Really laughed. The last time they'd stayed up late talking about something that mattered. The last time either of them had felt *seen*.

That night, Ryan asked Lauren the question: "What's one dream you have that I haven't asked about?"

She cried. Not because the question was hard—but because she couldn't remember the last time he'd asked.

She told him about the pottery class she'd been thinking about for two years. How she drove past the studio every week and imagined what it would feel like to create something with her hands again. How she'd convinced herself it was silly. Selfish. A waste of time.

Ryan signed her up the next day.

Three months later, Lauren came home from class with clay still under her fingernails and a light in her eyes he hadn't seen in years. She talked for an hour about glazes and firing techniques and the bowl she was making. And Ryan realized something: he'd fallen in love with her all over again.

Not because of the pottery. Because he'd remembered what it felt like to champion her. To pursue her. To make space for the parts of her that needed room to breathe.

And when Lauren asked Ryan the same question a week later— when she asked about *his* dreams—everything shifted.

They started hiking on Saturday mornings. They planned a weekend trip to a city they'd never visited. They stayed up late talking about what they wanted the next ten years to look like instead of just surviving them.

Their marriage didn't just survive. It came *alive*.

Building the Rhythm of Adventure

This doesn't need to be complicated or expensive. Start simple and build from there:

- Try something new once a month (a new restaurant, a hike you've never taken, a class together, or even a different route home).
- Plan experiences, not just routines.
- Ask about dreams regularly and find small ways to support them.
- Say "yes" more often than you say "no."

Not reckless. Intentional. Adventure is not about intensity. It's about aliveness.

Here's a thought.... Make an Effort Tonight.

Don't wait for the perfect moment or a big vacation.

Tonight, look your spouse in the eyes and ask one simple question: "What's one small adventure we could say yes to together in the next thirty days?"

Then listen. Dream a little. Decide on one thing—no matter how small—and put it on the calendar.

It might be a picnic in the park, trying a new recipe together, taking a drive with no destination, or finally signing up for that dance class you've both joked about. The size doesn't matter. The intention does.

Because every shared "yes" is a step away from complacency and back toward the alive, growing marriage God designed for you.

Your marriage doesn't need to be perfect. It needs to be pursued.

The rhythm of adventure is waiting to be rebuilt. Your spouse is worth the chase. Your future together is worth the adventure.

Time to make a move - Tick Tok.....

1. **When did you last feel truly "alive" together?**

   Identify what made that moment stand out—novelty, laughter, or a shared challenge—and bring more of it into your routine.

2. **What's one dream your spouse has that you haven't asked about lately, and how can you support it this month?**

   Ask, listen, and take one small action to show your support.

3. **Where has comfort replaced pursuit in your marriage, and what's one new adventure you could try together this month?**

   Notice old patterns and pick something new to experience together, even if it's small.

CHAPTER 14

THE RHYTHM OF GRATITUDE

If gratitude is lacking in your marriage, you can feel it in the silence at the dinner table. The way you avoid eye contact. The heaviness in your chest when you hear their car pull into the driveway. Your marriage hasn't exploded—it's just gone numb. And the worst part? You can't remember exactly when you stopped seeing them as a gift and started seeing them as the problem.

At the beginning of marriage, you noticed everything. The way she smiled when she was nervous. The way he remembered how you took your coffee. The small sacrifices, the inside jokes, the unique way your spouse saw the world. You felt lucky. Grateful. In awe that this person chose you.

Then time passed.

You started noticing what was missing instead of what was there. The effort fell short. The words that weren't quite right. The habits that once charmed you now annoy you more.

Without realizing it, you began to see your spouse more as a problem to manage than as a gift to cherish.

The Invisible Shift

This is the shift most couples never name, yet it quietly changes everything.

It's not the loss of love. It's not the loss of commitment. It's the loss of awe—the deep sense of "I can't believe I get to do life with this person."

Gratitude builds a culture of appreciation and joy in a marriage. When that culture fades, everything starts to feel heavier. Small issues loom larger. Tension rises faster. Patience runs shorter.

What you focus on, you magnify. And in marriage, what you magnify eventually shapes how you treat each other.

What Gratitude Actually Does

Gratitude doesn't ignore real problems. It simply puts them in perspective.

Without gratitude, you see flaws first. With gratitude, you see value first.

That single shift changes how you speak, how you respond, and how you love.

If you see your spouse as frustrating, inconsistent, or lacking, you respond with irritation, criticism, or distance. If you see them as a gift, as valuable, as someone worth fighting for, you respond with patience, honor, and renewed effort.

Same person. Different lens. Completely different marriage.

The Problem: Gratitude Doesn't Maintain Itself

Gratitude requires ongoing intentional effort. Without deliberate practices to sustain it, couples drift from appreciation into resentment. Life gets loud, stress is constant, and unless you intentionally look for what is good, your mind will naturally focus on what is wrong.

So if you want a different outcome, you need a different rhythm.

Building a Culture of Gratitude

This isn't about occasional appreciation or forced positivity. It's about creating a consistent pattern that reshapes the atmosphere of your home.

Here's how to build it:

1. **Notice Intentionally** — Train your eyes to see value instead of defaulting to criticism. Look for effort, growth, small wins, and character traits—even the subtle ones. Especially the subtle ones. What gets noticed gets reinforced.

2. **Say It Out Loud** — Unspoken appreciation has zero impact. Your spouse cannot feel what you only think. Say it simply and sincerely: "I appreciate how patient you were with the kids tonight." "Thank you for working so hard for our family—I see it." "I love the way you make me laugh even on hard days."

Simple words. Powerful impact.

3. **Write It Down** — Keep a gratitude journal for your spouse. Once a week, write down three specific things you're thankful for about them. Share one or two during your next date night or quiet moment. This small habit builds a powerful culture of honor over time.

Scripture calls us to this rhythm again and again: "Give thanks in all circumstances; for this is God's will for you in Christ Jesus" (1 Thessalonians 5:18).

Gratitude is not optional for the follower of Christ—it's an act of obedience and worship that spills over into every relationship, especially marriage.

Lucy heard Ben's car pull into the driveway and felt her shoulders tense. Another evening of careful distance. They moved through the kitchen like roommates—him at the counter, her loading the dishwasher, neither making eye contact. The air felt thick. Ben set down his keys, exhaled slowly, then turned toward her. "Lucy." She looked up, guarded. "Thank you for handling the kids this week while I was buried at work. I saw how patient you were when things got loud, and I don't say it enough—I'm grateful." Her hands stilled on the plate. Something in her chest loosened. She met his eyes, and for the first time in days, her voice softened. "Thank you for noticing."

And just like that, the heaviness lifted. Ben stepped closer, and Lucy didn't pull away. They finished dinner standing near each other instead of across the room. Later, they laughed at something the kids said—a real laugh, not the polite kind. For the first time all week, they felt like partners again, not opponents. That's what five minutes of genuine gratitude produced: the return of each other.

When you stop seeing your spouse as a gift, you don't just lose appreciation—you lose *them*. You stop seeing the person you married and start seeing a collection of failures and unmet expectations. They become a problem to manage instead of a soul to know.

Let's be honest. Gratitude feels easy when things are going well. But what about when you're frustrated? When your spouse isn't showing up well? When tension fills the air?

This is exactly when gratitude matters most.

Gratitude is not based on perfection. It's based on perspective. Choosing to see value when it's harder to find is what strengthens your marriage long-term. It's a quiet act of faith and leadership.

The Hard Truth

If you don't intentionally practice gratitude, you will unintentionally build resentment. There is no neutral ground— no "coasting" in marriage. Every single day, you are either moving toward your spouse or away from them. You're either appreciating or accumulating. And the scary part? Most couples don't realize which direction they're going until they're already too far down the road.

Final Question & Challenge

Be honest with yourself right now: Do you regularly express appreciation to your spouse… or do you mostly point out what's wrong?

One builds a connection. The other slowly erodes it. And over time, that difference becomes everything.

Tonight, start rebuilding the rhythm.

Before you go to bed, look your spouse in the eyes and tell them one specific thing you're grateful for about them— something real, something recent. Then ask them to do the same for you.

Make it a habit. Protect it. Watch how a simple rhythm of gratitude begins to soften hearts, restore awe, and breathe fresh life into your marriage.

Because your spouse is still a gift. Even on the hard days. Especially on the hard days.

The rhythm of gratitude is one of the most powerful ways to keep love alive—because what you treasure, you protect. And what you protect, you keep.

Two Different Marriages

One couple walks into the kitchen and notices the coffee already made, the kids' lunches packed, the effort their spouse put in before dawn. Their first thought is *I'm lucky*. When tension rises, they remember who they married—not just what went wrong today. They say, "Thank you for staying patient with me this week. I know I've been stressed, and you didn't have to be that kind." The words are specific. The tone is soft. Their spouse feels seen, not managed. Problems still exist—money is tight, schedules are chaotic, parenting is hard—but they face them together. Challenges don't define the marriage because appreciation is the foundation. At the end of a long day, they look at each other and still see a gift. Tired, imperfect, but treasured.

Another couple walks into the same kitchen and notices the dishes still in the sink, the mess on the counter, everything their spouse didn't do. Their first thought is *Of course*. When tension rises, it's just more proof they were right to be frustrated. They say, "You never listen when I'm talking." "You always leave things half-done." The words are vague accusations. The tone is sharp. Their spouse feels attacked, not loved. Problems become proof that something is fundamentally broken. Every disappointment confirms what they already believe: their spouse isn't enough. At the end of a long day, they look at each other and see a stranger. Tired, distant, barely holding on. They've forgotten what they once saw in each other, and now they're just surviving in the same house.

Same struggles. Same pressures. Same imperfect people. But one marriage is being built on gratitude, and the other is being eroded by resentment. The difference isn't circumstances—it's the daily rhythm of what they choose to see.

TALK ABOUT IT

1. **Do you notice your spouse's efforts or flaws more? When did that change?**

   Many couples find this shift is gradual and hardly noticeable. Discuss when appreciation faded into criticism, and what caused it. Identifying this pattern is key to reversing it.

2. **What did you once appreciate about your spouse but now overlook—and why should you remind them?**

   We tend to overlook daily moments like making coffee, caring for family, or sharing a laugh. This week, notice and appreciate one of these simple things.

3. **When did you last say, "I appreciate you for..." to your spouse? What if you did it weekly?**

   Speaking gratitude changes relationships; regular appreciation shapes culture. If it's been a while, you're not alone—your marriage is affected. Try making specific appreciation a weekly habit.

CHAPTER 15

THE RHYTHM OF INTIMACY

"The two shall become one flesh..." — Genesis 2:24

This chapter explains why intimacy fades, what to do when emotional and physical connection get out of sync, and how to rebuild a rhythm that honors both of you. We'll start with a familiar moment of distance, listen in on a turning-point conversation, and end with a simple framework you can use this week—so "one flesh" becomes a lived experience, not just a verse you agree with.

- How emotional and physical disconnection feed each other

- A conversation most couples avoid—plus a 4-step script to have it safely

- A shared rhythm (not a quota) that protects intimacy through real-life seasons

The distance didn't arrive with arguments or slammed doors. It accumulated—missed moments, rushed conversations, tired touches—until one night it finally got named.

"I don't feel as close to you," Rebekah said.

Ethan nodded. "I've felt that too—for a while."

147

That moment is more common than most couples admit. Sometimes it surfaces as an emotional complaint; sometimes as a physical disconnect. Underneath is often the same ache: two people who still love each other, but have stopped building the closeness that "one flesh" requires.

Think of Ethan and Rebekah as an early warning sign. Now let's look at what happens when that snapshot becomes a pattern—and what it looks like to break the silence and rebuild connection with intention.

Intimacy is more than sex. It's a shared life—emotional, spiritual, and relational—expressed in the way you choose each other.

- Emotional: sharing your inner world, your fears, your dreams
- Spiritual: connecting on a soul level, sharing values and purpose
- Relational: choosing each other daily, prioritizing time together

When one thread weakens, everything feels off. The whole fabric starts to unravel.

"Sometimes I don't feel connected emotionally," she said, setting down her mug. "Like we're roommates instead of partners."

Ethan listened, really listened this time.

"And that affects everything else," she continued. "I can't feel close to you physically when I don't feel close to you emotionally."

Physical and emotional intimacy are inherently connected rather than distinct categories. Many couples attempt to separate sexual activity from emotional connection, yet these aspects are designed to complement each other: emotional security enhances desire, and physical closeness strengthens unity. Neglecting one invariably undermines the other.

Avoidance increases relational distance, while silence leads to unspoken assumptions, unresolved resentment, and unmet expectations. However, deliberate efforts can restore connection—through open communication, thoughtful actions, and consistent presence.

A Cycle That Feeds on Silence

Look at this couple—Steven and Jessica—were stuck, not because they didn't love each other, but because they never talked about intimacy.

The pattern was predictable: Steven wanted more frequency. Jessica needed more emotional connection first. He'd initiate; she'd feel pressured and pull back. He'd feel rejected and stop trying. She'd feel unwanted and withdraw further—repeat.

Neither of them named it. Both of them felt it.

Underneath the silence was fear.

Steven feared that if he admitted how rejected he felt, Jessica would hear him as selfish. He carried quiet shame: *What's wrong with me that I can't just be okay with this?*

Jessica feared that if she told the truth—that his touch felt like pressure, that she was exhausted—Steven would conclude she was broken or didn't love him. She carried her own shame: *Why can't I just want this?*

Both feared they couldn't meet the other's needs—and that their own needs were unreasonable. So they stayed silent, because naming it felt more dangerous than enduring it.

It was especially hard when their child was young—privacy scarce, energy thin, resentment growing in the small gaps of daily life.

Jessica ended her days depleted—giving to everyone else, then trying to offer whatever was left at home.

By the time their child was asleep, they were both empty.

Physical intimacy requires the same vulnerability as emotional intimacy. You can't build it on assumptions or sustain it on silence—you have to talk about it.

Steven came home with a results-oriented attitude, believing that taking action would solve everything. He thought that being more proactive was the answer, but Jessica was worn out—overwhelmed, emotionally spent, and exhausted. Despite his efforts to try harder and initiate more, it didn't help because Jessica was drained from daily responsibilities and the constant demands of caring for their young child. She felt over-touched, emotionally depleted, and completely exhausted.

The turning point came one night when Jessica finally said, "I need to tell you something I've been afraid to say."

Her voice shook. Steven braced himself.

"I feel like you only touch me when you want sex. And that makes me not want to be touched at all."

She said it quietly, almost apologetically—as if she was the problem. As if wanting affection without an agenda made her unreasonable.

Her hands were trembling. She couldn't look at him. Because saying it out loud meant risking everything—his anger, his defensiveness, his rejection. It meant admitting that the distance between them wasn't just exhaustion or busyness. It was something deeper. Something she'd been carrying alone for years.

And now it was out there. Exposed. Vulnerable. She had no idea how he would respond.

Steven's first instinct was defense. *That's not true. I do care about you.*

But he stopped—because he watched her eyes. The way she looked away after speaking. The way her shoulders folded inward, like she was bracing for impact.

She wasn't attacking him. She was breaking open.

She was finally saying something she'd been afraid to name, and he was about to make her regret it.

He realized in that moment: she had been brave enough to speak. And if he got defensive now, she would never speak again.

So instead, he asked:

"What would help you feel desired—not just wanted for sex?"

And she told him.

She needed:

- Affection that didn't lead anywhere
- Conversation that went deeper than logistics and their child's schedule
- To feel pursued emotionally, not just physically
- To know Steven valued her, not just her body
- Space to not be "on" for everyone—including Steven

And then Steven had to be vulnerable too.

"I need to tell you something I've been afraid to say."

She listened.

"I feel like I'm always the one initiating. And when you say no—or when you seem uninterested—I feel rejected. Not just physically. Like you don't want me."

She didn't get defensive. She didn't minimize it. She just said:

"I didn't know you felt that way. Tell me more."

And they finally had the conversation they should have had years earlier.

The one they'd been avoiding because they were too tired, too busy, too afraid.

Most couples avoid talking about physical intimacy, hoping the problem will solve itself.

If you can't talk about it, you won't fix it. Not because you're hopeless, but because you're avoiding the tool God gave you: honest words.

If you want this area to change, you need four things:

- **Honesty** about what you need
- **Vulnerability** about what you're afraid of
- **Safety** to say hard things without shame
- **Intentionality** to create rhythm, not randomness

When Desire Doesn't Match

Desire mismatch is common—and it's easy to start keeping score. One spouse wants more, the other wants less; both can feel exposed and misunderstood.

And here's what you need to understand first: **desire mismatch is rarely about incompatibility.**

It's usually about biology, circumstance, or unaddressed pain.

Desire is affected by:

- **Hormones** — pregnancy, postpartum, menopause, low testosterone
- **Medication** — antidepressants, blood pressure meds, birth control
- **Health issues** — chronic pain, fatigue, thyroid problems, pelvic floor dysfunction
- **Past trauma** — sexual abuse, assault, or painful early experiences that create fear or shutdown
- **Mental load** — the invisible weight of managing a household, children, schedules
- **Stress and burnout** — work pressure, financial strain, relational conflict

None of these mean something is fundamentally broken in your marriage. They mean you're human, living in a body, in a season, with a story.

And here's something many couples don't know:

There are two types of desire—spontaneous and responsive.

Spontaneous desire can feel instant: you see your spouse and want them. Responsive desire shows up *after* you start connecting—emotionally, physically, relationally. It needs context, safety, and warmth to emerge.

Many people experience responsive desire. That doesn't mean they don't want intimacy—it means they need the right conditions for desire to awaken.

When the higher-desire spouse doesn't understand this, pressure increases—and pressure kills responsive desire every time.

That doesn't mean you're doomed—it means you need a plan, some humility, and a lot of grace.

Here's what married couples need to understand:

The goal is not to meet in the middle mathematically.

The goal is to honor each other in covenant.

That means:

For the spouse who wants more:

You're not wrong for wanting intimacy. Physical connection matters. Feeling desired matters. But here's what you have to understand: **pressure doesn't create desire—it destroys it.**

When you initiate constantly, when every touch has an agenda, when you sulk or withdraw after being turned down, you're training your spouse to avoid you. You're making intimacy feel like one more demand on the day instead of a gift.

So what does pursuing emotionally (not just physically) actually look like?

- **Ask about their day—and actually listen.** Don't just wait for your turn to talk. Be curious. Be present.

- **Touch without expectation.** Hold their hand. Hug them in the kitchen. Kiss them goodnight—without it being a setup for more.

- **Serve them in ways that matter to them.** Do the dishes. Put the kids to bed. Take something off their plate.

- **Create emotional safety.** Don't criticize. Don't keep score. Don't make them feel like they're failing you.

- **Ask: "What helps you feel safe and desired?"** Then listen. Then do it.

You're not trying to manipulate them into wanting you. You're trying to create the conditions where desire can grow.

For the spouse who wants less:

You're not broken. You're not failing. But you do have a responsibility here.

Physical intimacy matters to your spouse—not because they're shallow or selfish, but because it's how they feel connected, loved, and chosen. When you avoid, withdraw, or shut down without explanation, they feel rejected. Unwanted. Like they're too much.

So how does one move forward?

Understand your own patterns. What happens inside you when you feel pressured? Does your body tense up? Do you feel resentful? Guilty? Numb? Name it. Then share it—not as an accusation, but as information.

"When you initiate every night, I start to feel like I'm failing you. And that makes me want to avoid you."

"When I'm touched all day by the kids, I need space before I can be close to you."

"I want to want this, but my body doesn't cooperate right now. Can we figure this out together?"

Communicate honestly about you needs

- "I need 20 minutes to myself after the kids go to bed before we connect."
- "I need you to help me feel like a person, not just a mom."
- "I need affection that doesn't always lead to sex so I can relax into your touch."

Initiate sometimes—even when you don't feel like it. This isn't about performing or faking. It's about covenant. It's about saying, "You matter to me, and this matters to you, so I'm choosing to show up."

Responsive desire means you might not feel it until you start. So start. Create the conditions. Light a candle. Put on music.

Let yourself be present. Desire often follows action—it doesn't always precede it.

Ask: "What would make this feel more connected for both of us?" Then be willing to try.

But here's the hard question nobody wants to ask:

What if only one spouse wants to work on this?

What if you're reading this, ready to try, and your spouse dismisses it? What if they refuse the conversation, mock your vulnerability, or insist nothing needs to change?

That's not a desire mismatch. That's a covenant problem.

You can't force someone to care. You can't make them try. But you can name it. You can ask for help—counseling, pastoral support, honest conversation. And you can decide what you're willing to live with and what you're not.

Because marriage is a covenant—and covenant requires two people who are willing to show up and trust God to do the heavy lifting.

And here's the part nobody likes hearing:

Physical intimacy is part of covenant marriage—and neglecting it has consequences.

That does *not* mean you get to demand sex, pressure your spouse, or punish them when they say no. And it also does *not* mean you get to disappear, avoid, or withhold as a way to control the relationship. Covenant calls both of you higher: love, honesty, and responsibility.

It's not just biological. It's spiritual. It's relational. It's part of the one-flesh union God designed.

But it also shouldn't feel like:

- An obligation you resent
- A chore you endure
- A transaction you perform
- A weapon you withhold

It should feel like:

- Connection you cultivate
- Intimacy you protect
- Vulnerability you share
- Covenant you honor

So how do you get there?

You make it a rhythm.

Not random. Not reactive. Intentional.

A weekly rhythm means reserving time to connect, which varies by life stage:

- Newborns, School-age kids, Empty nest, High stress/travel, Health challenges

Daily affection — touch, closeness, non-sexual intimacy that builds safety

This is the glue. A kiss in the morning that lasts longer than two seconds. Holding hands while you watch TV. A hug in the kitchen that isn't rushed. Sitting close on the couch instead of on opposite ends. A hand on the shoulder. A back rub with no agenda. Touch that says, "I like being near you," not "I want something from you."

Regular check-ins — "How are we doing in this area?" (not avoiding the conversation)

These don't have to be formal or heavy.

The goal isn't to critique or pressure. It's to stay connected, to name what's true, and to adjust together instead of drifting in silence.

Adjusting for seasons — understanding that stress, kids, health affect desire (grace, not guilt)

Pregnancy and postpartum are not the same as your honeymoon phase. A wife recovering from childbirth needs tenderness, patience, and non-sexual affection—not pressure to "get back to normal."

A husband on new medication that affects libido isn't rejecting his wife—he's navigating a body that doesn't respond the way it used to. That requires compassion, not shame.

A season of grief—loss of a parent, a miscarriage, a job loss—will affect desire. You don't ignore intimacy, but you also don't demand it stay the same.

The rhythm adjusts. The commitment doesn't.

When you build rhythm into physical intimacy—It stops feeling like pressure and becomes a priority.

The spouse who wants more doesn't feel rejected. The spouse who wants less doesn't feel pressured. Because you're both showing up intentionally.

Not perfectly. But faithfully.

Making It Intentional Without Making It Mechanical

Some couples worry:

"If we schedule it, won't it feel forced?"

"Doesn't that kill spontaneity?"

Here's the truth:

Intentionality is not the enemy of intimacy. Neglect is.

Scheduling isn't mechanical; it protects what's important. It means valuing each other and making your relationship a priority, not leaving connection to chance.

A set rhythm allows for spontaneity, playfulness, and presence. The routine gives space—what happens in it is up to you.

Without rhythm, you wait for the perfect moment, often too tired or stressed, leading to rejection, guilt, and growing distance.

With rhythm, there's no pressure or guessing. You can prepare emotionally, safeguard your time, and consistently show up for each other, deepening your connection with every shared moment.

The Spiritual Dimension

Physical intimacy extends beyond biological aspects; it also encompasses theological significance. As stated in Genesis 2:24:

"Therefore a man shall leave his father and his mother and hold fast to his wife, and they shall become one flesh."

The concept of "one flesh" signifies more than mere physical union; it embodies a unified life, covenant, and relationship.

This union is characterized as:

- **Exclusive**
- **Sacred**
- **Vulnerable**
- **Intentional**

Engaging in physical intimacy within marriage is not merely about fulfilling a need. It demonstrates commitment to a covenant, reflects core principles of the gospel, and fosters unity. Therefore,

- It holds spiritual significance,
- Contributes to marital strength,
- Impacts one's broader influence,
- And warrants purposeful attention rather than disregard.

The Slow Fade

We've sat with countless couples who described this exact moment.

Take David and Lydia. They were high school sweethearts who married young. In the early years, they couldn't keep their hands off each other. They planned surprise dates, left love notes, and stayed up late dreaming about their future. Passion came naturally.

Then life happened.

Kids. Careers. Mortgage. Sports schedules. Exhaustion. They worked hard to "win" each other in the beginning, but once the ring was on the finger, the pursuit quietly stopped. They assumed security meant they no longer had to try as hard.

David later admitted, "I thought marriage meant the chase was over. Instead, I stopped chasing the woman I loved most."

Lydia felt it too. "We became roommates who shared a bed and a last name. The fire didn't go out in one night—it just slowly burned down to embers because no one was tending it."

What Actually Kills the Fire

It's rarely one big thing. It's the accumulation of small, repeated choices:

- You stop protecting time together.
- You stop communicating with depth and curiosity.
- You stop trying new things and creating fresh memories.
- You stop expressing genuine appreciation.
- You stop actively pursuing each other.

Sound familiar? These are the same rhythms we've already talked about in this book. That's not a coincidence.

The fire doesn't fade randomly. It fades when the rhythms that feed it disappear.

A large number of couples overlook gradual changes in their relationship, as the deterioration does not occur suddenly. There are distinct behaviors that serve as indicators of emotional distancing prior to reaching a critical point.

The following signs may warrant attention:

- **Emotional engagement declines.** Conversations shift from personal feelings to logistics, reducing emotional awareness.

- **Physical affection becomes routine or fades.** Spontaneous gestures disappear, and touch feels transactional or is absent.

- **Discussion of aspirations stops.** Talks about hopes and fears give way to practical matters, making the relationship more business-like than romantic.

- **Date nights lose meaning.** They're often filled with talk about kids or work instead of nurturing the relationship.

- **Little acknowledgment.** New looks, tough days, or achievements are frequently overlooked, so recognition is lacking even when together.

- **Humor avoids vulnerability.** Jokes deflect serious issues, limiting deep connection out of fear of conflict or rejection.

If you're recognizing yourself in any of these, don't panic. Awareness is the first step. The drift is real—but it's also reversible.

You Have to Keep the Chase Alive

This next part might feel uncomfortable.

Have you ever thought, "I shouldn't have to try this hard anymore. We're married."

Wrong.

You don't stop pursuing your spouse because you "got" them.
You pursue them *because* you chose them—and that choice is
meant to be renewed every single day.

The Song of Solomon never shows the lover settling into
complacency. Even after the wedding, the pursuit continues
with passion and delight: "Arise, my love, my beautiful one,
and come away" (Song of Solomon 2:10). The chase doesn't
end at "I do." It deepens.

Security without intentionality leads to complacency. And
complacency always leads to disconnection.

Intimacy Is More Than Physical

Most people hear "fire" and immediately think only of physical
intimacy. That's part of it—but only part.

True intimacy in marriage is layered:

- Emotional intimacy (feeling known and understood)
- Relational intimacy (sharing life as best friends)
- Spiritual intimacy (praying and growing in faith
  together)
- Physical intimacy (the beautiful gift of sexual
  connection)

When the first three areas are neglected, the physical one inevitably suffers too. You can't feel close in the bedroom if you feel distant in everyday life. That's not rejection. That's reality.

The Role of Effort

Here's a hard but freeing truth:

Feelings follow investment. Not the other way around.

Many couples make the mistake of waiting until they *feel* passionate before they act. That's backward.

Here's why: Your brain is wired to create associations through repeated experience. When you consistently show up—through touch, attention, meaningful conversation, acts of service— your brain begins to build neural pathways that associate your spouse with safety, pleasure, and connection.

Every time you reach for your spouse's hand, hug them in the kitchen, ask a real question and listen to the answer, your brain releases oxytocin—the bonding hormone. The same chemical that flooded your system when you first fell in love. It's not magic. It's neuroscience.

The more you invest through small, repeated actions, the more your brain rewires how you perceive and feel about your spouse. What felt distant begins to feel familiar again. What felt obligatory begins to feel desirable. Not overnight—but gradually, consistently, as you keep showing up.

You don't need to feel it first. The feeling comes *as* you invest.

That's why so many say, "We just don't feel it anymore." The real issue is usually, "We stopped doing the things that created those feelings in the first place."

You act first—through consistent time, communication, gratitude, and adventure—and the feelings of closeness and desire gradually return.

Keeping your relationship strong takes intention but isn't complex.

- Prioritize Connection, Add Variety, Show Affection

The Hard Truth

If you don't intentionally keep the fire alive, it will go out. Not because your marriage is doomed—but because that's just how neglect works, every time.

Moving from Guilt to Hope

If you're reading this and recognizing yourself in the drift, don't spiral into condemnation. The drift is *common*—and it's *reversible*. It's not evidence that you're a failure or that your marriage is broken beyond repair.

It's evidence that you're human. That life got busy. That you stopped protecting what you assumed would always be there.

The gap between where you are and where you want to be isn't a canyon—it's a series of small, repeatable choices. And those choices start to rewire not just your habits, but your heart.

Here's what neuroscience and behavioral psychology confirm: new investment creates renewed feeling. When you consistently show up—through time, touch, conversation, pursuit—your brain begins to associate your spouse with safety, pleasure, and connection again. The feelings you're waiting for don't come first. They follow the investment.

Six Months Later

Remember Ethan and Rebekah from the beginning of this chapter? The couple sitting at the table, naming the distance that had quietly accumulated between them?

I checked in with them recently. Things aren't perfect—they're quick to say that. There are still exhausting weeks. Still moments when one of them has to initiate the conversation the other is avoiding. Still nights when they're too tired for anything more than holding hands on the couch.

But something fundamental has shifted.

"We talk now," Rebekah said. "Not just about schedules and logistics—about *us*. About how we're doing. About what we need. It doesn't feel scary anymore."

Ethan nodded. "And I pursue her differently now. I ask about her day and actually listen. I touch her without it always leading somewhere. She knows I see her—not just as my wife, but as *her*."

They protect Friday nights now. Sometimes it's a date. Sometimes it's just sitting together after the kids are asleep, talking about something deeper than the week's to-do list. Sometimes it leads to physical intimacy. Sometimes it doesn't. But they show up.

"The biggest change?" Rebekah paused. "I feel chosen again. Not just loved in theory—but pursued. Like he still wants *me*, not just what I can give him."

That's what rhythm does. It doesn't create a fairy tale. It creates a marriage where both people feel seen, safe, and desired—because both people are choosing, consistently, to show up.

This is available to you too.

Not through perfection. Not through waiting until you feel like it. But through the same choice Ethan and Rebekah made: to stop drifting and start tending the fire again.

One conversation. One touch. One protected moment at a time.

TALK ABOUT IT

1. **Where are we aligned or misaligned?**

   Reflect on our emotional, spiritual, and physical connection. What feels close, and what feels distant now?

2. **What issues are we avoiding, and what is the impact?**

   Identify any unspoken concerns—whether about intimacy, desire, or fears.

3. **What makes us feel desired and safe?**

   Specifically, what actions or words help each of us feel genuinely wanted and comfortable being open?

CHAPTER 16

FIGHTING FOR "TEAM US"

There are two kinds of fights in marriage.

One kind tears you apart. The other brings you closer.

Believe it or not, the majority of couples don't know they are choosing one of them—every single time conflict shows up.

They think a fight is just a fight—tension that either gets resolved or doesn't. But the truth is bigger: the way you fight determines whether conflict becomes a wedge between you or a bridge that deepens connection.

Every argument is a choice.

Most couples make that choice unconsciously—defaulting to old patterns, old defenses, and old fears.

Without intention, you'll keep repeating what you learned— rather than building what you want.

The question is: *which direction will you go?*

The Default: Fighting Against

When tension rises, instincts take over.

You defend. You attack. You self-protect.

Suddenly, the goal shifts from "Let's fix this" to "Let me prove I'm right."

The argument becomes about:

- Who said what
- Who did more (or less)
- Who's at fault

You end up on opposite sides of the same marriage, keeping score like opponents in a game neither of you can really win.

I watched this play out with Chris and Nicole.

They argued for years about one thing: how Chris handled discipline with their teenage son.

One night, their son crossed a boundary. Chris snapped—voice raised, tone sharp. Nicole said, "I wish you'd just talk to him instead of yelling."

That's all it took.

"Don't question my parenting," Chris said, voice cold. "I'm doing the best I can."

"I'm not questioning you—I'm trying to help," Nicole replied.

"Well, you're not. You're just criticizing. You always—"

"I always what? Tell me. What do I always do that's so terrible?"

"You undermine me. With the kids. With everything. Like I can't do anything right."

And there it was—seventeen years of resentment bubbling up in a single sentence.

Nicole's face changed. Not angry now—hurt.

"That's not fair," she said quietly. "And you know it."

But Chris wasn't listening anymore. He was defending.

"This is why I don't talk to you about these things. You always turn it into something about me."

Nicole opened her mouth to respond, then stopped. What was the point? He wasn't hearing her. He never did when he got like this.

They finished the conversation in silence. Went to bed facing opposite walls.

The parenting issue never got solved. But something else happened: another fracture formed. Another moment where they felt less like partners and more like opponents who happened to share a house.

Chris lay awake wondering if Nicole would ever see him as doing anything right.

Nicole wondered if she was just destined to feel unheard.

That distance sat between them for days. The kind of distance that doesn't announce itself with slammed doors or raised voices. Just... coldness. Politeness. Two people moving through the same space, careful not to touch the wound.

They'd had this fight before. Different words, same pattern. And every time it happened, the gap between them widened just a little more.

A few months later, the same issue came up again. Their son crossed a boundary. Chris wanted to respond immediately; Nicole wanted a calmer approach. The difference this time wasn't the topic—it was the posture.

Chris said, "I'm feeling disrespected and a little panicked. I don't want to explode—can we talk for five minutes before we decide what to do?" Nicole replied, "Yes. And I'm feeling afraid that we'll be harsh and regret it. Help me understand what you think needs to happen." Instead of trading accusations, they named their emotions, asked questions, and chose a plan together. The conversation didn't feel perfect—but it felt safe. And they walked away more united than they started.

The Problem with Winning

You can win the argument and still lose the relationship.

You can prove your point and damage trust.

You can be technically right... and still be completely wrong in how you handled it.

Because marriage isn't a courtroom. It's not about keeping score. It's about building something together.

If you're thinking, "That's us," don't feel condemned. Feel invited. The goal isn't perfection—it's progress, one conversation at a time.

Every conflict either strengthens or weakens your marriage over time. There's rarely neutral ground.

The Shift: Fighting for "Team Us"

Everything changes when you make this shift:

"It's not me versus you. It's *us* versus the problem."

It sounds simple. It's not easy.

Emotions run high. History gets dragged in. Pride screams for victory. But if you don't make this shift, you will keep repeating the same painful cycles—different issues, same destructive patterns, same painful outcomes.

Fighting for "Us" means the relationship itself is more important than who wins the moment.

Here's what most couples miss: in marriage, there's no such thing as a "personal win" that doesn't touch the relationship. If Team Us doesn't win, you both lose. You might win the point, the tone, the debate, the proof—and still lose peace, trust, tenderness, and connection.

Fighting for "Us" means I care more about *who we're becoming* than what I'm trying to prove. It means I'd rather be close than be crowned. It means I'm willing to lay down my pride, my perfect argument, and my need to be right—because protecting the relationship matters more than protecting my ego.

This is the posture Scripture calls us to—"quick to listen, slow to speak, slow to anger" (James 1:19), and looking to the interests of our spouse, not just our own (Philippians 2:3–4).

So in the middle of conflict, ask a better question than "How do I win?" Ask: **"What does Team Us need right now?"**

Same team. Same goal. Same fight. When your words and tone match that reality, conflict stops feeling like a threat—and becomes a tool God uses to mature you and bind you together.

- **We name the problem, not the enemy.** The problem is the problem—your spouse is not.
- **We don't keep score.** Scorekeeping turns partners into opponents.
- **We protect the relationship while we pursue the solution.** Tone, timing, and respect matter.

How to Fight for Each Other

Those principles sound good on paper. But what do they actually look like when you're standing in your kitchen at 10 p.m., exhausted, and the conversation is about to go sideways?

Here they are in action:

The first thing you need to do—before anything else—is **say it out loud.** Not just think it. Say it: "We're not enemies. We're on the same team." It sounds simple, almost too simple. But naming the reality you want changes the posture you bring. You're not squaring up like opponents. You're turning shoulder-to-shoulder to face the problem together.

That shift—from adversaries to allies—is what makes the next three steps possible. Without it, you're just using techniques. With it, you're building something.

Step One: Slow It Down

Most of the damage in conflict happens when things move too fast. Words fly. Voices rise. You say things you can't take back.

So the first move is to pause. Breathe. Pray if you need to. Give yourself ten seconds before you respond. It's the difference between reacting and responding—and that difference can save your marriage.

I've watched couples learn to say things like, "I'm getting worked up right now. I don't want to say something I can't take back. Can we take ten minutes and come back to this?" That one sentence—spoken with humility instead of heat—can stop a fight from becoming a wound.

Slowing down doesn't mean avoiding the issue. It means you care enough about the outcome to handle it well.

Step Two: Listen to Understand

Once you've slowed down, the next step is to actually listen—not to defend yourself, not to prepare your comeback, but to understand your spouse's heart.

This is harder than it sounds. Because when someone you love is upset, your instinct is to explain, justify, or correct. But that's not listening. That's self-protection.

Real listening sounds like this: "Help me understand what you mean by that." Or, "What I'm hearing is that you felt dismissed when I didn't ask about your day. Did I get that right?"

Notice what's happening there. You're not agreeing or disagreeing yet. You're just making sure you actually understand what they're saying. You're repeating it back. You're asking follow-up questions. You're treating their perspective like it matters—because it does.

Step Three: Take Responsibility

This is where most couples either turn the corner or stay stuck.

Instead of focusing only on what your spouse did wrong, ask yourself: *What did I contribute to this?*

Even if you think you're only 10% at fault and they're 90%, own your 10%. Say it out loud. "You're right—I did interrupt you. I'm sorry." Or, "I can see how my tone hurt you. That's on me."

Small ownership lowers the temperature. It opens the door. It signals that you're not just trying to win—you're trying to heal.

And here's the thing: you can't skip any of these steps. If you slow down but don't listen, you're just delaying the explosion. If you listen but don't take responsibility, your spouse will feel heard but not believed. And if you try to own your part without slowing down first, it'll come out defensive or sarcastic.

These three steps work together. They build on each other. And when you get all three right, something shifts.

A couple I know—let's call them Mark and Jenna—had been fighting about money for years. Same script, different day. Mark would make a purchase without telling Jenna. Jenna would find out and feel blindsided. Mark would get defensive. Jenna would shut down. Repeat.

One night, it happened again. Mark bought new golf clubs. Jenna saw the charge on their account.

But this time, before the old pattern could take over, Mark paused. He didn't defend the purchase. He didn't explain why it was a good deal. He just said, "You're right. I should have talked to you first. I'm sorry."

Jenna, instead of unloading, took a breath. She asked, "Help me understand—what made you think this was okay without checking in?"

Mark admitted he felt controlled when it came to money, like he couldn't make any decisions. Jenna admitted she felt scared because they'd been burned before by impulse buys.

They weren't agreeing yet. But they were finally *understanding* each other. And from that place, they could actually solve the problem instead of just trading accusations.

That's what these three steps do. They turn conflict into connection.

But here's the hard truth: none of this works if you're not willing to do it when it's hard.

The Hard Truth

If you don't learn how to fight well, you'll slowly tear down what you're trying to build—not because you don't love each other, but because you don't have the tools.

Without the right tools, even good intentions can turn conflict into destruction.

When It Feels One-Sided

What if you're trying to fight for "Us" and your spouse is still fighting against you?

You can't control them. But you can lead.

Leadership in marriage looks like consistency when it's hard. Keep choosing grace. Keep listening. Keep owning your part. Over time, covenant love can change the atmosphere of your home—even if it takes longer than you want.

One important note:this chapter is about normal marital conflict—not situations where there might be abuse. Intimidation, threats, or repeated emotional or physical harm falls outside of what we are talking about. If that's part of your story, don't carry it alone. Get outside help immediately from a trusted pastor, friend or counselor.

Final Question & Challenge

Be honest with yourself right now: When conflict shows up in your marriage, are you trying to win the argument… or are you trying to build the relationship?

That single choice is shaping your marriage more than you think.

Tonight—if tension rises (or the next time it does)—pause and ask: "Is what I'm about to say fighting *against* my spouse… or fighting *for* us?"

Then choose the higher road. Say it if you need to: **Same team. Same goal. Same fight.**

Your marriage is worth fighting for. Not against.

Choose to fight well. Choose to fight together. Choose to fight *for* "Us."

And when you don't fight well—and you will sometimes—your next lifeline is forgiveness.

Forgiveness is one of the most powerful and necessary rhythms in any Christian marriage. Without it, small offenses accumulate into bitterness, trust erodes, and emotional distance grows—even in "pretty good" marriages. With it, marriages can heal, deepen, and reflect the gospel in profoundly beautiful ways.

- **The goal of conflict isn't winning—it's strengthening the relationship.** Every fight is either tearing you apart or building you up over time. There's rarely neutral ground.

- **You can't control how your spouse fights, but you can lead by example.** Consistent covenant love changes the atmosphere—even when it takes longer than you'd like.

- **Unresolved conflict doesn't disappear—it escalates.** What you don't address now will resurface louder, sharper, and more destructive later.

- **Fighting well requires tools, not just good intentions.** Without a framework for healthy conflict, even couples who love each other deeply can slowly tear down what they're trying to build.

1. **How does conflict usually unfold in your marriage?**

    Be honest about your real patterns when tensions rise.

2. **What fears come up for you during conflict— rejection, misunderstanding, being controlled?**

    Name your fear and ask your spouse what helps them feel safe during disagreements.

3. **In your last disagreement, did you act for the relationship or just to win?**

    What words or actions could have improved the outcome?

CHAPTER 17

THE RHYTHM OF FORGIVENESS

Marriage joins two imperfect sinners under one roof. Hurt, disappointment, and failure are inevitable. You will sin against each other—sometimes in small ways (sharp words, forgotten promises), sometimes in devastating ones (betrayal, neglect, or broken vows).

Unforgiveness is slow poison. It replays the offense, hardens the heart, and suffocates intimacy. As one couple shared in their testimony, holding onto hurts turned their home into a pressure cooker of silent tension until they learned to release them to God.

Forgiveness, by contrast, is freedom. It releases the bondage that was formed by the offense. It mirrors how God has forgiven us and opens the door to reconciliation, healing, and renewed closeness. Ephesians 4:32 commands it clearly: "Be kind to one another, tenderhearted, forgiving one another, as God in Christ forgave you."

Jesus ties our forgiveness of others directly to our experience of God's forgiveness (Matthew 6:14-15). Refusing to forgive isn't just relational—it's spiritual. Yet He also models lavish, repeated forgiveness: when Peter asked how often to forgive,

Jesus replied: "seventy-seven times" (Matthew 18:22)—
meaning without limit.

Forgiveness does **not** mean:

- Pretending the offense never happened ("forgive and
  forget" instantly).
- Removing all consequences or skipping the hard work
  of rebuilding trust.
- Staying in unsafe situations (abuse requires wisdom,
  boundaries, and often outside help).

It **does** mean releasing the right to keep punishing or holding
the sin over your spouse's head. It cancels the debt in your
heart, even when feelings lag behind.

Unforgiveness is a clenched fist—tight, tense, protective.
Forgiveness is the slow, painful opening of the hand so healing
can flow again.

A Real Story of Forgiveness in Marriage

For years, a wife carried wounds she didn't know how to name.
Her husband's unfaithfulness and inconsistency left her feeling
like she was living on shifting sand—never sure when the next
disappointment would hit. She remembers one night sitting
alone at the kitchen table long after everyone was asleep,
staring at a cold cup of coffee, feeling the weight of resentment
pressing on her chest.

She had stopped expecting anything from him. She had stopped praying for him. She had even stopped praying for herself.

One morning, while reading Scripture, she sensed God confronting her—not with condemnation, but with clarity: *"Your bitterness is costing you more than his sin ever did."*

Forgiveness, she realized, wasn't about excusing him. It was about freeing her heart so God could heal what had hardened.

She began small. A whispered prayer. A choice not to replay the offense. A decision to confess her own coldness. Day by day, her heart softened. Her husband noticed the shift—not instantly, but unmistakably. Conviction grew in him. Repentance followed.

Their marriage didn't snap back overnight. But forgiveness created space for God to rebuild what bitterness had been slowly destroying. Today, they describe their marriage as more honest, tender, and Christ-centered than they ever imagined possible.

Stories like theirs—and countless others marked by betrayal, addiction, or emotional neglect—remind us that God's grace doesn't just repair what's broken. It resurrects what looks dead.

Now, I know forgiveness feels impossibly hard when you're in the middle of real hurt. But this couple's story—the softened heart, the husband's repentance, the restored joy—isn't a miracle that happened *to* them. It's what happens when someone actually practices forgiveness, one day at a time. That same transformation is available to you.

Practical Steps to Practice Forgiveness

Forgiveness begins as a decision and grows into a rhythm. Here's how to cultivate it:

- **Acknowledge the Hurt Honestly** — Name it to God and to your spouse. Suppressing pain doesn't help; grieving it does.

- **Release the Debt to God** — Decide to stop rehearsing the offense in your mind. Hand the "right to punish" over to Him. This is where the cross becomes personal—Christ canceled *your* massive debt, so you can release your spouse's smaller one (Colossians 2:13-14; 3:13).

- **Pray for Your Spouse (and Yourself)** — Ask God to bless them and heal you both. Prayer softens your heart faster than almost anything else. Over time, it replaces resentment with compassion.

- **Confess and Seek Reconciliation** — Own your part first (even if small). Confess sins to each other and pray together (James 5:16). Forgiveness opens the door; repentance and changed behavior rebuild trust.

- **Replace Bitterness with Gratitude and Grace** — Return to rhythms like daily expressions of appreciation. Speak life-giving words (Ephesians 4:29). When old hurts resurface, choose again to forgive—seventy-seven times if needed.

When Hurt Runs Deep: Safety First

In serious cases—infidelity, addiction, abuse—safety must come first. This isn't negotiable. If you're in an unsafe situation, reaching out to a trustworthy counselor, pastor, or mental health professional isn't a sign of weakness or lack of faith. It's a wise and courageous step to protect yourself and your family.

Forgiveness and Reconciliation Aren't the Same

Here's something important to understand: true forgiveness can happen in your heart as an act of obedience to God, even when reconciliation isn't yet possible. But full reconciliation—rebuilding trust and restoring the relationship—requires something more. It takes time, genuine repentance, clear boundaries, and often professional support. Forgiveness is what you do in your heart. Reconciliation is what you build together, and it can only happen when both people are committed and safe.

Forgiveness Doesn't Mean No Consequences

Let's clear up something that confuses many couples: **forgiveness does NOT mean there are no consequences.**

You can release someone from the debt they owe you in your heart—that's forgiveness—while still maintaining wise boundaries as trust is being rebuilt. Forgiveness releases bitterness. Boundaries protect what needs to be protected.

Here's what this looks like in real life:

If your spouse has lied repeatedly, forgiveness doesn't mean you automatically believe everything they say without question. You forgive the past lies, but you also require honesty and transparency moving forward. That's not punishment—that's wisdom.

If your spouse has been financially irresponsible—hiding purchases, racking up debt, making major decisions without you—forgiveness doesn't mean you immediately open joint accounts again and hand over the credit cards. You forgive the betrayal, but you also establish accountability structures and rebuild fiscal responsibility together first.

If your spouse has been emotionally withdrawn or dismissive for years, forgiveness doesn't mean they get full access to your heart again without addressing the root issues. You forgive the hurt, but you also need to see consistent effort, vulnerability, and changed patterns before you reinvest emotionally at the same level.

Here's the critical distinction:

- **Punishing** (withholding forgiveness): *"I'll forgive you when you've suffered enough. When I feel like you've paid for what you did."*
- **Boundaries** (forgiving with wisdom): *"I forgive you completely, AND I need to see changed behavior and rebuilt trust before I reinvest fully in this area."*

Forgiveness is about releasing your right to punish. Boundaries are about protecting what needs to be protected while trust is being rebuilt.

This isn't unforgiveness dressed up as wisdom. It's wisdom dressed up in grace.

You can forgive someone fully in your heart—releasing all bitterness, choosing not to bring it up repeatedly, praying for them genuinely—and still require them to earn back trust through consistent, changed behavior over time.

In fact, that's exactly what healthy reconciliation looks like.

Forgiveness opens the door. Changed behavior and time rebuild what was broken. Both are necessary. Neither one alone is enough.

The Gospel at the Center

Forgiveness in marriage isn't powered by willpower alone—it's fueled by the cross. While we were still sinners, Christ died for us (Romans 5:8). He forgave us fully, freely, and at infinite cost. When we remember how much we've been forgiven, extending that same mercy to our spouse becomes not just possible, but a joyful overflow of grace.

A strong marriage isn't the union of two perfect people—it's the union of two good forgivers. When both spouses live this way, conflicts become opportunities for deeper intimacy rather than division. The home becomes a living picture of the gospel: brokenness met with relentless, covenant love.

If unforgiveness has taken root in your marriage, confess it to God. Choose to release one specific hurt. Ask your spouse for forgiveness for any time you've withheld it. Watch how the Holy Spirit brings fresh life where bitterness once lived.

Every offense creates an emotional IOU. Forgiveness is tearing up the debt—not pretending it never existed but refusing to collect on it. That's the Gospel Story.

Your marriage is worth fighting for—with grace, not grudges. Forgiveness isn't always easy, but it's always worth it. It reflects the heart of the One who forgave you first.

1. **What wound are you still carrying, and how is it shaping the way you see your spouse today?**

   Name it. Don't soften it. Don't justify it. Just tell the truth.

2. **What would releasing bitterness look like in your marriage this week—not in theory, but in one concrete action?**

   Identify the obstacle. Decide if it's worth the cost of holding onto it.

3. **Where do you need to confess your own part— not to take blame that isn't yours, but to own what is?**

   Humility heals what pride keeps broken.

CHAPTER 18

THE RHYTHM OF TRUST

"Love... keeps no record of wrongs." — 1 Corinthians 13:5

Trust doesn't usually break all at once.

Sometimes it does.

But more often—It erodes.

Slowly. Quietly. Over time.

"I don't think it's one thing," Rebekah said.

Ethan nodded.

"Yeah... It's been building."

Small disappointments.

Missed follow-through.

Unspoken frustration.

Each one feels manageable in the moment.

But over time—

They accumulate.

And what accumulates...

Eventually affects trust.

"I don't feel as secure as I used to," Rebekah admitted.

Ethan listened carefully.

Not defensive. Not reactive.

Just present.

That mattered.

Because rebuilding trust begins with listening.

But then she continued, and the weight of it became clear.

"You said you'd call me back that Tuesday," she said quietly.
"After your meeting. You didn't. And I know it's small, but I'd
been waiting to hear from you. I needed to know you were
thinking about me."

Ethan felt something tighten in his chest.

He remembered that Tuesday. He'd forgotten. Completely.
And when she'd mentioned it later, he'd brushed past it—*I was
busy, I'm sorry*—as if the apology erased the fact that he'd
made a promise and broken it.

"And then there was my birthday dinner with my parents,"
Rebekah continued. "You said you'd remember to make the
reservation. I reminded you twice. And you forgot. I had to call
and scramble at the last minute."

He wanted to defend himself. *I've been stressed at work. I have a lot on my mind.* But he stayed quiet.

Because he was beginning to see something he hadn't wanted to see.

"It's not that you're a bad person," Rebekah said, her voice steady but sad. "It's that these things keep happening. And each time, I tell myself it doesn't matter. But it does. Because every time you forget, or you say you'll do something and don't, it tells me something."

"What does it tell you?" Ethan asked, though he thought he already knew.

"That I'm not a priority. That my needs don't matter enough for you to follow through. That I can't count on you the way I used to."

The words landed hard.

Because she was right.

He hadn't been thinking about how his forgetfulness affected her. He'd been thinking about his own stress, his own problems that seemed overwhelming. He'd been operating as if his broken promises were just small oversights—inconveniences, not betrayals.

But they were accumulating.

And they were eroding something essential.

Trust.

The kind of trust that says: *I know you'll show up for me. I know you're thinking about me. I know I matter.*

Ethan realized, sitting across from her in that moment, that he'd been slowly teaching her the opposite.

"I haven't been thinking about this the way I should have," he said finally. His voice was quiet. "I've been thinking about my own stuff. Not about what it does to you when I don't follow through."

Rebekah nodded.

"That's what I need you to understand," she said. "It's not about perfection. It's about showing me that you care enough to try. That I'm worth remembering."

Trust is not just about: Big betrayals.

It's about:

Consistency. Reliability. Follow-through.

It's built in small moments—

Repeated over time.

"So how do we rebuild it?" Ethan asked.

Rebekah answered slowly.

"Not all at once."

That's key.

Because trust is not rebuilt through words.

It's rebuilt through **Consistency.**

— STEP-BY-STEP TRUST REBUILD

1. Acknowledge Clearly

No minimizing. No deflecting.

2. Take Ownership

No excuses.

3. Create Transparency

Nothing hidden.

4. Stay Consistent

Over time. Because trust is not restored in a moment—it's rebuilt choice by choice, action by action, day by day.

(Seth & Laura)

Let me tell you about Seth and Laura—a couple who, on the outside, seemed to have it all together. But the truth is, their relationship went through a season where they almost lost each other. And it wasn't because they stopped loving one another. It was because trust, that invisible thread that holds us together, quietly unraveled until it became a wall between them.

It didn't happen overnight. It started with little things. Seth began traveling for work more often. Laura would ask him to call when he landed. He always said yes, but then would get caught up in meetings and forget. He'd promise to be home by six, but would show up at seven, often without so much as a text. Nothing intentional, nothing dramatic—just little slips, inconsistency, and forgetfulness.

What Seth didn't realize was that trust isn't built on grand gestures or big moments. It's built on the everyday—on whether you do what you say you'll do when nobody's watching and it doesn't seem to matter much.

Eventually, Laura stopped asking him to call. Seth thought her silence meant she'd accepted his schedule, but in reality, she'd stopped expecting him to follow through. And when you stop expecting someone to show up for you, something precious starts to die in the relationship.

On the surface, they were still kind. They still said, "I love you." But a guardedness crept in. Laura was polite but distant. When Seth suggested spending time together, she hesitated— protecting herself from more disappointment.

About eight months into this pattern, Seth finally asked what was wrong. Laura simply said, "Nothing," but her eyes said everything. Eventually, she breathed out the truth: "I don't feel secure with you anymore." That hit Seth hard. He loved her. He was working hard to provide for their family. But that wasn't enough.

And here's the thing about trust—it's not about effort in general. It's about following through on the specific promises you make. Laura said, "I don't know if you're thinking about me when you're not here. You say you will, and then you don't. And I've stopped believing you will."

Seth's first instinct was to fix it with grand gestures—a romantic weekend, flowers, heartfelt letters. And Laura appreciated it. But it didn't restore trust. Because trust isn't rebuilt by big moments. It's rebuilt by small, repeated acts of faithfulness.

That's when everything shifted. Seth realized he was asking for forgiveness—which Laura gave—but he hadn't earned back her trust. Forgiveness happens when someone chooses to let go of being angry. Trust, though, is what happens when someone believes you'll do what you say you'll do. Those are two different things.

So Seth made a decision—not a dramatic one, but a simple commitment: he would text Laura every time he said he would. Not just sometimes, but every time. Even if he was busy. Especially if he was busy.

The first week, he texted from the airport. Laura seemed surprised. The second week, he called at lunch as promised. She was cautious but hopeful. By the third week, something began to change—she started believing him again.

But here's what was hard: Seth had to do this over and over, for months. It was humbling. He felt constantly tested, like he had to earn back something he thought he already had. But that's what rebuilding trust requires. Laura needed to know—not just believe, but know—that she mattered enough for him to follow through. That his word meant something.

And slowly, over weeks and months, the wall between them came down. Not because of one perfect moment, but because of a thousand small moments where Seth did what he said he would do.

Now, five years later, their relationship is stronger than ever. The trust they rebuilt is even deeper than before—because it was built intentionally, through choice and consistency, not just passion or feeling.

If you're in a season where trust has eroded the way it did for Seth and Laura, remember: it can be rebuilt. But it requires patience, humility, and doing the small things faithfully—even when no one's watching and it feels like it doesn't matter.

TALK ABOUT IT

1. **Which promises have you broken in your marriage, and how has that affected your spouse's trust?**

   Note any patterns and listen to your partner's perspective without making excuses.

2. **How well do you follow through on commitments in your marriage?**

   Identify where you've relied on vague effort instead of specific follow-through, and honestly assess any gaps between your words and actions.

3. **What small, consistent action can you take this week to rebuild trust?**

   Pick something measurable—like calling when promised—and stick to it every time, focusing on reliability over apologies or big gestures.

CHAPTER 19

THE RHYTHM OF LEGACY

Your marriage is not just about you.

It never was.

It impacts far more than the two of you sharing a home, a bed, and a last name. Your marriage sends ripples into:

- Your children
- Your extended family
- Your church community
- Your friends and coworkers
- Generations that haven't even been born yet

Whether you realize it or not, people are watching. They are learning. They are absorbing what a marriage is supposed to look like—by watching *yours*.

The Marriage Your Kids Will Repeat

This is one of the most sobering truths in marriage.

Your children are far more likely to repeat what they *saw* in your marriage than what they were *told* about marriage.

They are forming their understanding of:

- What love looks like on ordinary Tuesdays
- How conflict is handled (or avoided)
- Whether forgiveness is real or just words
- How a husband treats his wife and how a wife honors her husband
- Whether marriage is a safe place of joy or a tense place of survival

They notice everything.

They notice when you speak kindly to each other, even when you're tired. They notice when you fight fair instead of tearing each other down. They notice when you laugh together, pray together, and pursue each other. They also notice the cold silences, the sarcastic jabs, the eye-rolls, and the emotional distance.

One father told me with tears in his eyes, "I realized my son was learning how to treat his future wife by watching how I treated his mother. That scared me into changing."

The Generations You'll Never Meet

But here's what that father didn't fully realize yet: his faithfulness wasn't just shaping his son's future marriage. It was shaping his grandchildren's understanding of love. His great-grandchildren's capacity for commitment. His great-great-grandchildren's belief that covenant is something worth keeping.

You are planting seeds in soil you will never see harvested.

Moses understood this when he gathered Israel and said, "Hear, O Israel: The Lord our God, the Lord is one. Love the Lord your God with all your heart and with all your soul and with all your strength. These commandments that I give you today are to be on your hearts. *Impress them on your children. Talk about them when you sit at home and when you walk along the road, when you lie down and when you get up*" (Deuteronomy 6:4-7).

Notice the rhythm Moses describes—sitting at home, walking along the road, lying down, getting up. In other words: *in the ordinary moments of daily life*. That's where legacy is built. Not in the grand speeches you give your children about marriage, but in how you speak to your spouse when you're tired on a Tuesday evening. Not in the lectures about commitment, but in whether they see you choose each other again and again when it would be easier to choose distance.

Your marriage is teaching a curriculum whether you intend it to or not.

And when you stay faithful through the hard seasons—when you choose to love even when you don't feel like it, when you forgive even when it costs you something—you're demonstrating to everyone watching that *covenant is real.* That promises can be kept. That faithfulness is actually possible in a world that has largely stopped believing in it.

The prophet Malachi understood the weight of this: "The Lord is the witness between you and the wife of your youth. You have been unfaithful to her, though she is your partner, the wife of your marriage covenant... So be on your guard, and do not be unfaithful" (Malachi 2:14-15). God calls Himself a *witness* to your marriage covenant. And so is everyone else.

Your faithfulness gives them permission to be faithful. Your perseverance shows them that perseverance is possible.

One woman told me, "I was ready to leave my husband. We'd been struggling for years. But then I watched my parents celebrate their 40th anniversary, and my dad said something I'll never forget: 'There were seasons I wanted to quit. But I'm so grateful I didn't, because I would have missed the best years of my life.' That's when I realized—I was about to walk away right before my breakthrough. My parents' faithfulness literally saved my marriage."

That's the ripple effect of covenant-keeping. Your children are watching to see if promises can be trusted. Your friends are watching to see if love can last. And when you stay—when you fight for your marriage instead of against each other—you're preaching a sermon more powerful than words.

The Spiritual Magnitude of What You're Building

Let's be clear about what's actually at stake here.

Your marriage is a witness to the character of God.

Paul writes in Ephesians 5 that marriage is a mystery that reflects Christ and the church—which means every act of sacrificial love, grace, and reconciliation in your marriage is demonstrating the gospel in real time.

This is the magnitude of what you've been entrusted with.

The writer of Proverbs understood this: "A good person leaves an inheritance for their children's children" (Proverbs 13:22). We often read that as financial inheritance, but the greatest inheritance you can leave isn't money—it's a model of faithfulness. It's the gift of watching two imperfect people choose each other, forgive each other, and build something beautiful together despite the brokenness.

You're planting trees whose shade you'll never sit under.

And that's exactly the point.

A Word to Those Who Feel the Weight of What's Been Lost

If you're reading this and feeling the weight of conviction—if you're realizing that your marriage hasn't been the model you wish it had been—I want you to hear this clearly:

It's not too late.

Maybe you've spent years in emotional distance. Maybe your children have witnessed more conflict than covenant. Maybe you've modeled cynicism instead of commitment, survival instead of safety.

The enemy would love for you to believe that the damage is done, that the legacy is set, that there's no point in changing now.

But that's a lie.

The same God who redeems broken people redeems broken legacies.

The same grace that covers your sin covers your failures as a spouse. The same power that raised Jesus from the dead can resurrect a marriage that feels dead.

Paul writes to Timothy: "Set an example for the believers in speech, in conduct, in love, in faith and in purity" (1 Timothy 4:12). Notice he doesn't say, "Set an example if you've been perfect." He says set an example—period. Because the most powerful example isn't perfection. It's *repentance*. It's change. It's two people who realize they've been getting it wrong and decide to start getting it right.

Your children don't need to see a flawless marriage. They need to see a *faithful* one. And faithfulness includes the humility to admit when you've been unfaithful and the courage to start again.

One couple I know gathered their adult children and said, "We need to apologize. For years, we modeled a marriage that was more about coexistence than covenant. We were in the same house but not truly together. We're sorry for what we showed you. But we want you to know—we're changing. And we're inviting you to watch us build something different."

Their kids wept. Because what they witnessed in that moment was more powerful than if their parents had been perfect all along. They witnessed *repentance*. They witnessed *humility*. They witnessed two people who loved their children enough to admit their failures and loved God enough to pursue something better.

The Call

So here's what I'm asking you to consider:

What if your marriage isn't just about your happiness? What if it's about something far bigger—a calling, a stewardship, a sacred trust?

Your marriage is one of the most spiritually significant things you will ever be invited to embrace.

God has entrusted you with something precious: the opportunity to show the world what covenant looks like. To demonstrate that faithfulness is possible. To plant seeds of love and commitment that will grow into forests of legacy.

People are watching. Your children are learning. Generations are being shaped.

The question is: what will they see?

Will they see two people who stayed when it was hard? Who forgave when it was costly? Who chose each other again and again, not because it was easy, but because covenant matters?

Or will they see two people who gave up when it got difficult? Who let distance become normal? Who settled for coexistence instead of fighting for connection?

You get to decide.

Not perfectly. Not flawlessly. But faithfully.

And that faithfulness—imperfect, stumbling, grace-covered faithfulness—will ripple further than you can imagine.

Your marriage is building a legacy.

Make it one worth inheriting.

TALK ABOUT IT

1. **Consider how your marriage influences those around you—children, friends, or your community.**

   Honest self-reflection helps identify what example is truly being set.

2. **Reflect on the message your marriage sends and whether your actions match the legacy you hope to leave.**

   Effective legacies require deliberate choices and sustained growth.

3. **Choose one positive behavior to model consistently in your marriage.**

   Legacy is built through repeated, visible actions—define a clear behavior, such as respectful communication or quality time, and commit to it so others can learn from your example.

CHAPTER 20

A BLESSING FOR THE JOURNEY

Let's slow down for a moment.

You've made it to the final chapter—not because the work is finished, but because the real journey is just beginning.

Wherever you are right now—whether your marriage is struggling deeply, feeling steady but stuck, or already growing stronger—there is more available to you than you can see in this moment.

Not because you and your spouse are perfect. Not because you've finally mastered all the rhythms. But because God is present, He is far more committed to your marriage than you are.

You Are Not Building Alone

From the very first page of this book, we've talked about intentional rhythms, honest self-examination, and the daily choices that shape a thriving marriage. But here's the truth that anchors everything:

You are not doing this by yourself.

God is with you.

He is strengthening you when you feel weak. He is guiding you when the path feels unclear. He is sustaining you when the effort feels heavy. He is redeeming what feels broken and breathing fresh life into what has grown dim.

Isaiah 41:10 gives us this beautiful promise: "Fear not, for I am with you; be not dismayed, for I am your God; I will strengthen you, I will help you, I will uphold you with my righteous right hand."

That promise is for your marriage, too.

There will be hard days ahead—days when old patterns try to creep back in, when tiredness wins for a moment, when one of you feels like giving up, or when life throws something unexpected at you. In those moments, remember this:

You are not just maintaining a relationship. You are building something meaningful. Something worth fighting for. Something that can grow, heal, strengthen, and become far more than it is today.

A Blessing Over Your Marriage

As we close these pages, receive this blessing for the journey ahead—not as empty words, but as a prayer spoken over you and your spouse from the heart of God's Word:

- May you not drift. May you choose—every day—to live with intention instead of settling for "fine."

- May you not grow comfortable in distance. May you fight for connection, for understanding, and for the beautiful rhythms that keep love alive.

- May you pursue each other with fresh passion, honor each other with genuine respect, and grow together in grace and truth.

- May your home be marked by: covenant love that doesn't keep score, forgiveness that sets hearts free, gratitude that magnifies what is good, and adventure that keeps your marriage young at heart.

- May you build something that lasts—not because you are strong, but because you are anchored in the One who never leaves.

- May your marriage become a living testimony of what's possible when two imperfect people say "yes" to God's design.

- May the Holy Spirit empower you on the days when you feel weak. May grace cover you on the days when you fall short. And may joy rise again on the days when the fire feels dim.

- May your love for one another be marked by unfathomable peace and joy.

- May it be the kind of love that causes others to pause—to notice—to wonder what makes it different.

- May your eyes still light up when your spouse walks into a room.

- May laughter remain easy, even at the simplest jokes.
- May you never lose the quiet joy of simply being together.
- May you be found—years from now—still wildly in love.
- May the rhythms you choose today echo far beyond your lifetime.
- May your life together become a gift—not only to one another—but to everyone around you.
- And when your children grow...may their prayer be:
- **"Lord, let me love like mom and dad."**

Take the next small step. Protect the next sacred moment. Speak the next kind word. Extend the next act of forgiveness. Choose the next rhythm.

Your best days in marriage are not behind you. They are still ahead—because God is with you, and He is writing a beautiful story with your lives.

You've got this. Not because you're enough on your own, but because the God who began a good work in you will carry it on to completion (Philippians 1:6).

Here's to your marriage. Here's to your legacy. Here's to the beautiful, imperfect, grace-filled journey ahead.

So here's to the miracle of us.

Here's to a love that lasts.

And here's to the rhythms of marriage.

With love, faith, and belief in what your marriage can become—

Bill & Jennsey McGee

RHYTHMS OF MARRIAGE

STRENGTHENING YOUR RELATIONSHIP
TO THE BEAT OF GOD'S DESIGN

www.rhythmsofmarriage.org